NINE LITTL

MW00412389

A composite of a psychotherapist's sessions with Ron – with nine different personalities – the son of a serial killer and sexual abuser. Ron's Multiple Personality Disorder is activated and documented during his sessions, when he becomes nine distinctly different children, each a victim decades ago. His story is completely true and factual.

DAVID PETER JOHNSON, MSW, MPH, LCSW

Copyright © 2009 by David P. Johnson, MSW, MPH, LCSW

Cover design by Cathy Grames

All rights reserved.

No part of this book may be reproduced in any form or by any electronic or mechanical means including information storage and retrieval systems, without permission in writing from the author. The only exception is by a reviewer, who may quote short excerpts in a review.

Printed in the United States of America

First Printing: March 2010

REG. NO. TXu 1-625-823

INTRODUCTION

I have been a therapist for more than four decades and much of my work, by choice, is with the chronically mentally ill. I work a lot with Schizophrenia, Bi-polar Disorder, Personality Disorders, and major depression. Of course, addiction problems are involved also. I do long term therapy, lasting for several years if necessary.

Rarely, I come across a patient such as Ron, who suffers from a type of Dissociative Identity Disorder (DID), commonly known as Multiple Personality Disorder. Ron has nine separate and distinct personalities, all children reflective of the ages at which specific trauma occurred. His story is 100% non-fiction. Ron's story is, up to date, and one can see at the book's conclusion exactly how he has progressed and to what extent he is in control of his "Nine little Ronnies."

Dedication

This book is dedicated to Ron and Barbara – Ron for his "trailblazing" motivation

geared to educate therapists, psychiatrists and patients regarding Dissociative

Identity Disorder (multiple personality disorder) – Barbara for her standing by Ron

while he suffered so intensely with mammoth divisions within himself.

Ron's courage and determination stand as a guidepost for those whose identities

have been sacrificed by brutalities during childhood.

Therapist

I will feel your feelings.

I will know your thoughts

I will understand you deeply,

experience your fears

accept your rage,

with compassion

and genuine empathy.

Allow me to touch your heart,

And maybe you will dare

to LIVE once again!

David Peter Johnson

*   *   *

Chapter 1

Many people who suffer from mental illness feel very alone in their daily struggle to cope. For these people group therapy is not simply a way for them to vent or share their experiences, but the group atmosphere can serve as a community in itself, with group members helping other members as neighbors in a community might. Also, for many of my patients the group therapy sessions can be the only reason for them to get out of their house each week, which can be therapeutic in itself.

In today's group session, Angie is encouraging another member to come to a peaceful resolution in a family matter. Ron also encourages peaceful resolution. Ron and Angie both suffer from Dissociative Identity Disorder, or DID. In Ron's case, this disorder lay dormant for thirty-five years, and only developed as the result of a head injury inflicted during a car accident.

I ask Ron to talk about the events leading up to his beginning therapy with me. The following is his story:

I was in a serious car accident last March. I was broadsided by a 4X4 pickup truck, which caused more than $12,000 damage to my car. At the time I thought I was unharmed except for a headache sustained when my head hit the side window. A couple of days later I began having severe neck pain, which was traced to a herniated disk in my neck. I had trouble with pain and weakness in both arms bad enough to keep me from working at my job as a bowling center mechanic, which involves heavy lifting. I ended up having surgery to repair the injury in May, but I healed very slowly and was restricted to lifting 5 to 10 pounds or less for several months. I spent all summer and into the fall unable to work at my job and unable to contribute to anything around the house. I became very depressed and a royal pain to be around.

It was during this period, March through September, that some very odd things began happening to me. I would attempt to do something at home – straightening up the study, for instance – and I'd be sure that I'd done the work, but then would go back into the room and discover nothing had been touched. At first, I reasoned that I must have simply dreamed of working, but after a few instances like this, I began to worry. I became very irritable and my wife Barbara has said she spent all summer "walking on eggshells."

Then one Saturday, all of us were in particularly bad moods. Barbara and her mother got into an argument over something, and I heard her mother cast a couple of disparaging remarks her way. This brought me into the fray to find out what was going on, and her mother and I began shouting at each other. The subject matter varied, but the main gist was that "no one was doing anything" and she was tired of putting up with our crap.

I'm not sure what happened next. I have precious little memory of the rest of that day. The bottom line is that I somehow snapped and ended up shoving her into her recliner. How we came to be on the porch (we started the shouting match in the kitchen), and how I ended up grabbing her is still a mystery. Barbara and I were kicked out of the house and I suddenly was a very different person from the one who woke up that morning.

I started displaying behavior that frightened Barbara greatly. After several medical tests, including brain scans, we concluded that whatever was happening to me was psychological. After two months in a day hospital, I came to meet Dave, and here we are.

Ron began coming into my office holding a stuffed animal and talking like a small child. He was assuming the personality of a boy about age nine. Ron has nine distinct personalities in all, each personality representing himself at a particular age during his childhood. For example, the boy referred to as "Nine" is Ron, dissociated to that age in his life. The same is true for the eight other personalities. Each of these children have come out separately in therapy sessions and at home.

The following page contains a table that lists all of Ron's personalities in the order in which each child came out. The child's name and/or age are also given in a corresponding manner. The name each personality gave to Barbara when he came out is also shown. While dissociating, each child saw Barbara as a mother figure, not as a wife. Also listed and corresponding to each personality are characteristics unique to each child.

RON'S NINE DIFFERENT PERSONALITIES

Order	Name	Calls Barbara	Characteristics
1	Ronnie "Nine" or sometimes "The first one"	Aunt Barbara	Has food hidden, because dad punished him by not allowing him to eat. He has a comic book collection and likes to play with balls. He loves hamburgers and French fries. At this age he would hide under the house from dad after dad hit him.
2	Ronnie "Ten"	Aunt Barbara	Had bandaged eyes when first emerged, because of dad's car battery exploding in his face. Stumbled in on his mom and dad having sex and was tied to the bed to watch. Likes to listen to baseball games on radio and pet his puppy. Puppy was killed by another "mama" dog when dad wouldn't let Ron bring her inside.
3	Ronnie "Eight"	Aunt Barbara	Likes kites. Always thinks Barbara has come to visit rather than the other way around like all the other personalities do. At this age, dad first started drinking in front of family, instead of hiding it.
4	Eleven or "Head Kid" (HK)	Used to call her Aunt Barbara, now jokingly calls her Aunt Mama	Takes care of everyone. Can almost always be relied upon to tell Barb what "Uncle Ron" has been doing, unless intentionally blocked by one of the other personalities. Spent time in homemade shelter in the woods. Has a smile that lights up the room.
5	Ronnie "Seven" or "Rocket Kid " (RK)	Mama Barbara	Loves to blow bubbles and play with dogs. Can't understand why the others don't like his daddy because he remembers good things about dad
6	Ronnie "Twelve"	Warm Barbara	Is always cold, so likes to be covered with a blanket. Was shut in root cellar numerous times and also in spring house. Dad's punishments included making him dig ditches in the middle of the night and clean already clean items such as dishes and floors. Often hid in the woods.
7	Ronnie "Thirteen"	Safe Barbara or sometimes Warm Barbara	Always wants to be safe. Spent lots of time in the woods. Would set up "alarms" made from beer cans to let him know if anyone was coming. Always wants to be hugged
8	Ron "Fourteen"	Aunt Barbara	Likes to dance. Spent most of his time hanging onto Shadow, another personality. He is very concerned with the kids' safety.
9	Shadow	Barbara Mom	Twitches shoulders, cups his fingers to Barb's fingers. Very sensitive – always asking "Barbara Mom OK?" Writes left handed. Worries a lot that he has done something wrong. Used to be very angry. Says he was the one that shoved Barbara's mother.

The diagnosis of Dissociative Identity Disorder has gotten a "bad rap" because of psychopaths assuming the disorder, and using it in court by blaming the "other" personality for the theft or misuse of someone's credit card, etc...

*   *   *

Chapter 2

Today's session with Ron is fruitful. Last night he had a vision in which his father stood in front of him while he was sleeping. Ron does not suffer from hallucinations; this was strictly a one-shot deal. He was naturally frightened by this vision, but I reassured him that this does not mean he's crazy. I told him that I felt he is unconsciously working on his feeling towards his father. It is not surprising that this experience occurred. I encouraged him to have further visions of his dad and to take the opportunity to discuss his feelings with him in his dreams. Ron has to resolve these feelings, and I told him we would monitor them in individual and group therapy. His ability to discuss feelings of anger, and how that relates to the decline of dissociating into one of his other childhood personalities, what he calls "splintering," is a key factor. My feeling is that before the several personalities will integrate into one mature personality, Ron has an enormous amount of work to do discussing his feelings.

Ron reminds me that there is one individual in group who has the habit of muttering side comments to a close friend who usually sits next to him in group. This pisses him off and he wonders how to handle it. I told him that this is an excellent situation to practice expressing legitimate anger without dissociating. Other members of the group have witnessed the muttering and consider it a nuisance, but choose not to handle it directly. Ron is usually a mild-mannered person, but perhaps there is more to him than meets the eye.

Morning group is composed of both chronic patients as well as patients recently out of the hospital or day treatment. They are often in a state of psychic distress and/or trying to decide on proper types and dosages of medications. A few of them have great difficulty staying awake in group, because of heavy medications they are on. Today, both Donna and Guy are having difficulty staying awake. Group is small today because it has been snowing heavily all morning. Donna, Guy, Ron, George and Angie are present.

Ron is seeking help from the group, because he plans on telephoning his three siblings and discussing his sexual and physical abuse by his father. He has never broached the subject with them. His breakdown occurred only a few months ago, prior to which he did not recall the abuse. His memories were apparently shaken loose by the car accident. The group prepares Ron for the upcoming phone calls to his siblings. They caution him that at least one sibling will probably call him a liar and ask him why he is trying to dig up trouble. One of them may be thankful that he or she was not the only one to be abused or may simply tell him, "It's all in the past...get on with your life." Several people in the group have been through family sexual abuse, so they are helpful in preparing Ron for typical family responses.

Since Angie has been through such a family reaction, she is very supportive of Ron and speaks today for a long period of time about her family's denial. Today, all of Angie's "splinters" are one, and she is currently a well-functioning mother of three children. Angie simply warns Ron to be ready for trouble. I am asking Ron to secure the help of his wife when he makes the phone calls to his family members, since he is splitting off into several little Ronnies, and is going through a lot of emotional turmoil.

During the morning's group session Ron talks about the recently recovered memory of his father locking him in the family's well house for seven or eight hours. His dad told him if he got out before being let out, he would get beat up and later his mom would get a beating. Ron spent several hours beating snakes and insects off his head. Because this is a new memory, and we anticipate that more of his past will eventually come back to him, I suggest to him that when he get memories or flashbacks, he should record them in a notebook as soon as possible and we would go over each memory in our sessions.

Today, I again suggest to Ron that ideally, the only time he should be reliving dramatic memories is within the context of a therapy session. He agrees and he will try to cooperate. Ron explains one of his major dramatic experiences:

> *I was trying to locate my mother. She and I were very close. I searched the house and couldn't find her. I heard muffled sounds coming from my parents' bedroom. I couldn't make out the sounds. I opened the bedroom door and I saw my parents in bed. My father stood up and said that now that I had intruded, he was going to show me something. After tying me up, he tied mom up, with one arm and one leg to each post on the bed; then, he had sex with mom with me watching. I was about nine or ten and didn't know what they were doing. I thought he was hurting her. Mom told me not to be scared and that she wasn't being hurt. Dad punched mom in the face and told her to shut up. He then punched me in the chest hitting me real hard in an area that was healing from a fire that occurred when his car battery blew up all over me. I still had bandages all over my face at that time and some on my chest. He got me back on top of the bed, and told me to touch mom's breasts and vagina. I can't remember anything after that.*

I inquire if dad made Ron have sex with mom or him, but Ron can't remember anything further. However, Ron has had feelings that there is something he can't recall. Time is running out of the session, and I suggest to Ron that because we seem to be "on a roll," we should meet again in two days at 8:00 in the morning; he agrees.

During Ron's session I ask him to try to remain conscious when I see him attempting to drift off. His tendency is to dissociate, and I occasionally stop that process by my reminders. I reassure Ron that the more we can go over the details of his memories in sessions, the less he will need to do it in a dissociative fashion. This is theoretical and the outcome will determine if I am correct. Ron sometimes says that what we are doing feels okay, and he would like to continue with the process. The therapy sessions are not painless, but they end up being much less painful than losing consciousness out in public. For instance, in the past he has lost several hours at a time, woken up miles from home and did not know how he had gotten there.

After a period of time trying the previously mentioned method, it becomes obvious that Ron is dissociating while taking part in therapy. He repeats his memories speaking in the first person, as if he is back in a certain period of his childhood. At times, he appears to be in some type of trance. At the close of each session, when I say, "It's time to plan for our next meeting," Ron appears to "wake up" and I then reiterate what he has said while in the dissociative state. I give him several minutes to digest the information, because he has not been aware of what he has said. I offer him reassurance and tell him, "If you need to dissociate to get at painful stuff, that is perfectly okay with me."

There are times when Barbara, Ron's wife, attends his sessions and her presence allows Ron to speak more freely about certain issues because Ron's "splinters" have a trusting relationship with her. When she is here, he seems to "come back to himself" more readily and is comfortable having Barbara and I help him recall what has happened in the session.

*   *   *

Chapter 3

Tonight Barbara will be in the women's group for the first time. She will have the opportunity to discuss her feelings about helping Ron through his healing process. I am a strong believer in including family members in treatment. By helping a wife or other family member's feelings get expressed in a constructive way, it benefits the patient greatly.

Ron hasn't been able to work for months, so the family's finances have been weakened. By helping Ron deal with his feelings he will be ready to go back into the workforce sooner.

Much of tonight's women's group deals with supporting Barbara, in her dealing with her husband, Ron, who had switched personalities frequently over the weekend. He became himself at ages 9, 10, 11, 12, and 14. Barbara talked to Ron's individual personalities and reassured them. Barbara believes that Ron is regressing in order to help deal with his mother's recent death.

*　　*　　*

Chapter 4

Over the last couple of weeks, Ron has called several times to cancel sessions. Ron also asked his wife Barbara to call me to corroborate his stories about flat tires or other car trouble that kept him from therapy sessions. It is looking like Ron may be avoiding therapy sessions.

This particular morning I ask Barbara to tell Ron to come to my office today for his appointment even if he is very late due to some sort of circumstances that are delaying him. Ron shows up, and I make a comment to him that I will not feed into his need to avoid therapy by terminating him because he is not showing up. I tell him I could make a guess, based on his previous verbiage, about the incidents that are trying to come into focus, but I do not want to pollute his memory. Ron remembers his dad forcing him to touch his mother's breasts, but after that Ron remembers nothing. I remind Ron that we're going to see this through and that I'm not going to be angry if he misses appointments. I will be patient and be there for him, knowing the intense difficulty of the situation.

Ron is here today, trying to accurately remember his childhood. He can't understand why he has so few memories. Today he remembers his father's carbon monoxide suicide attempt. Ron remembers coming into the house with his mom, smelling the gas and trying to locate his father.

Ron urged his mom to leave home and escape from the cruelties of his father, but she couldn't do so because she felt it would be "killing him." From what we know so far, Ron's mom seemed to be a very kind person, but Ron has never been able to understand why his mother was never assertive enough to leave her husband.

Ron's dad finally died of heart failure. He was diabetic and had lung problems too. This was in 1986, and Ron's mom lived alone after her husband's death. One day, only a few years after Ron's father died, Ron's mother decided to let her half-sister come to live with her. It turns out that Charlotte was a lot like mom's deceased spouse – dictatorial and controlling. Charlotte was supposed to help Ron's mother with her loneliness. It didn't work out that way.

Ron's mother died in February of 2000. She had had a very high cholesterol level, and some blocked arteries. She lived with her half-sister Charlotte until about a year and a half before her death. While being treated in the hospital for abscesses on her kidneys, she told the nurses that she did not want to return to her own home that she shared with Charlotte, wanting to move in with her daughter Viola and son-in-law, who recently moved back into the area after living on the West Coast for several years. Her daughter took wonderful care of Mom, but it was apparent that Mom's time spent with Charlotte took a great toll, physically and emotionally.

Returning to the story of Ron's past, he remembers that at age 13 his mom announced that they could not leave and abandon his dad. Mom told Ron that she was afraid that Dad would kill himself if they left, but Ron suspected that Dad might kill Mom and him and try to say that they "ran off." At that time, Ron was seriously depressed and frustrated about the way that he was living and he got hold of his razor-sharp hunting knife and cut his two wrists in a superficial suicide attempt. After cutting himself, Ron realized that he couldn't abandon his mom in this way, so he bandaged himself up and went back to helping her survive in this meager existence. He realized that his killing himself would not hurt his father at all because he was such a "selfish, manipulating bastard."

As Ron matured from a skinny little boy into a slender teenage woodsman, his strength increased and one proud day he punched his father in the mouth with his right hand. Following this occasion, Dad became a bit wary of Ron and backed down against him for fear of being socked in the mouth again.

Ron's mom came from an abusive household; that's why Ron feels that she was so accustomed to abuse that her definition of what was normal was skewed. Mom allowed her half-sister to dominate her as well.

Ron is worried about his wife Barbara having another physical problem with her neck. Barbara fell a week ago; hitting her head on the edge of the sofa, and the neck injury began acting up.

In therapy, Ron is now working on his 13th year, when he tried to cut his wrists. At that time, Ron was greatly disappointed by Mom's refusal to run out on Dad. The gap Ron feels in his memory involves the rest of year 13. Ron got used to sleeping with one eye open, feeling that he had to be ready to protect his mom.

* * *

Chapter 5

Ron is no longer losing hours or days; his dissociations are far fewer. He is actually remembering incidents and not repressing them, therefore, he has more time and energy to help Barbara with household chores and to begin taking steps towards some kind of employment.

Ron describes "visions." He sees his dad in the doorway. He has taken my advice and has had imaginary discussions with his dad. Sometimes he will simply tell Dad to "go away" because he does not choose to have him in his life. In Ron's discussions with his dad, Ron is told "not to bother to get treatment for his illness because he is going to turn out to be a bum anyway." As Ron talks more and more, his vision becomes less solid and more translucent. Ron says, "My mind is giving me the opportunity to say things to my dad that I didn't dare say when I was a kid."

More everyday memories are coming back – some good memories. He remembers crawling under the house where his dog would go to have puppies. He would have to crawl under the house to get the newborn puppies out.

Nagging at the back of Ron's mind are indications that his dad had forced him to do terrible sexual things. I am careful not to suggest that anything happened. I do not want to make Ron remember anything in order to prove a theory of mine. Too many therapists get excited about the possibility of uncovering such things and manipulate the patient to imagine things that in reality did not happen. His memories have to be real, not trumped up to reinforce a therapist's theory.

Ron wants to go back to his home town to visit his brothers and his sister and discuss the trauma he has gone through. He thinks more light can be shed on his father's behavior by discussing such matters with his siblings.

Ron's 11-year-old "splinter" is a key manifestation of his trauma. This year seems to be a turning point in his life.

During Ron's eighth year, his father started drinking openly in front of the family. During this year, Ron's dad attempted suicide twice. Also this year, dad's favorite child, his first son went off to college. Ron was the youngest of the four kids, three boys and a girl.

Ron's dreams always have something to do with water, either a flood, a river overflowing, etc. He can't figure out why water is so often involved. One night he dreamt he was in medical school making rounds and the patient's room was filled with water. Also, dreams of a waterfall filling up a room are prevalent. He never remembers being scared, yet he wakes up suddenly.

With these dreams, he is losing sleep. "It is driving me crazy, this water thing." Ron did grow up around water, with a creek about 200 feet from his home. There were several lakes within half a mile from home, as well as millponds just a little further away.

At age twelve, Ron had surgery for a double hernia. He had been missing school a lot because of stomach pain resulting from the hernia. The ether that was used in the surgery caused bizarre feelings for a couple of weeks after the surgery.

It is great that Ron is recalling things. He lets it slip that "the second time Dad tied me up and made me watch him and Mom having sex ..." Ron didn't realize what he was saying until I stopped him, asking, "You mean he did this to you more than once?" Ron's mouth opens wide, astonished, and I say, "Ron, you just remembered that this perversion occurred more than once!"

Ron recently remembered that he was locked in the root cellar and the well house several times, not just once. Once Dad chased him, punched him in the gut and carried him over his shoulder to the root cellar. Dad said, "It is time for you to think about your behavior." This last incident occurred when he was twelve. When Ron was twelve years old, his next oldest brother was starting college and living on campus, so there was no one left at home who could protect him from Dad while Mom was away from the house.

The first time Ron was made to watch the sex, he couldn't see much from his position, but he could hear his parents making types of noises he had never heard before. One time when Ron was forced to watch his parents' sexual activities, he felt nothing but fear, and he remembers wishing his dad dead. Dad would taunt Ron, asking, "Is this what you want to see? You should try this sometime."

Ron went to college at age eighteen and had difficulty socializing, due to his level of anxiety. He lived in a dorm at the University of South Carolina. He was on a floor that did not allow visits from the opposite sex. This was in his freshman year. Later, he moved into a dormitory that allowed visitation from girls. His dates were few and far between. At twenty-one, Ron had his first acts of sexual intercourse. He doesn't remember any trauma occurring that was caused by his father's activities with him.

At age twenty-two, Ron met Barbara, his current wife. They got married when he was twenty-three. They had a healthy sex life prior to marriage. During relations with Barbara, Ron never thought back to Dad's perversions. He feels such memories had been completely repressed. Only during the past several weeks in therapy did Ron remember the incidents where he was tied to his parents' bed.

* * *

Chapter 6

In tonight's women's group, Barbara tells of the previous week's incidents with Ron and how he was switching personalities and becoming either seven-, eight-, nine-, ten-, eleven-, twelve-, and fourteen-year-old little Ronnies. When this happens, Barbara simply listens and encourages each "splinter" to express himself. A lot of each child's behavior is geared towards reaction to various threats from Dad.

Barbara is glad that Ron has scheduled a session between him, myself and her because she feels that Ron is getting ready to uncover some traumatic event that is very threatening to him. All the evidence from the little Ronnies points to this and she fears that what will come out is some form of sexual abuse.

This subject quite naturally, causes Betty and Kay to pay close attention in women's group because both of them were victims of sexual abuse by their respective parents. Betty remembers out loud how her mother took naked pictures of her at age eleven and passed them out to relatives. Betty's mother never gave those photographs back to her and she threatened to show the pictures to Betty's boy friend.

I ask Kay if she can talk to the point of her mother's sexual abuse of her. Kay willingly speaks about her version of sexual abuse at the hands of her mom when she was a child. All four kids – three boys and a girl – were sexually fondled by Mom. For years Dad denied this. The subject was never up for discussion in the family household and family therapy was out of the question.

The women's group members are mystified at listening to the role of the non-participating parent in these cases of group members' childhood sexual abuse. They understand the perpetrator's role clearly. The moms or dads in such situations tended to look the other way and chose to be unaware of the situation. The perpetrators are clearly the guilty parties, but the other parents' roles seem equally pathological, in a different way.

Recently, Barbara got a visit from Ronnie Twelve. It involved the root cellar again. This was only the first dissociation this week and currently it is never happening at any other place than at home or in this office, so perhaps we're doing something right.

Ron's wife Barbara is facing possible disc surgery. She also has a cataract that is causing problems, and this eye situation is not a common cataract problem because of her retina disease. She is under a great deal of stress.

Ron says, *"Dad treated me like a little kid. He was always laughing at me and mocking me. If we disagreed, he would ask me "What are you going to do about it?"*
Ron continues,

> *I had another dream with water in it. This one involved the harbor. There was this great big ship coming in to the dock too fast and it crashed into several boats. I had some kind of job there, but I don't know what kind of job. Somehow, in the dreams about water it's my fault; whatever is happening is my fault.*

There is a thirteen-year-old splinter who has come out at least twice. At thirteen, Ron was devastated by his mother's refusal to leave her husband. Ron says, "I went out to the woods with a hunting knife with the intention of cutting my wrists again, but I didn't follow through that time."

With each splinter that comes out, it is associated with one major event. For example, with eight-year-old Ronnie, what came out was seeing Dad for the first time drunk. The ten-year-old came out around the experience of the car battery blowing up in Ron's face when Dad was repairing the family car.

Ron states, "Eleven came out around the incident of Dad tying me up and forcing me to watch mom and him having sex, and him forcing me to touch my mom's breasts. He forced me various times to touch Mom in the vaginal area and in the breast area." I ask again. "Did your dad succeed in forcing you to have sex with your mom or him?" Ron's reply is, "I'm not ready to go there yet. There were so many times when I wanted to tell him to go to hell, but I couldn't stand up to him."

Ron's session today proves to be very meaningful. Ron says, "Something's out there that I need to deal with, but I don't know what it is." He sighs and takes deep breaths,

> *My dreams involve both Mom and Dad, but they are not sexual dreams – I just don't know – small scenes of hospital rooms, small scenes of the root cellar.*
>
> *I'm trying to be less unstable around Barbara, but I've been having panic attacks again. It may be anticipation of what's in my head that's trying to come out.*
>
> *I realize now that I felt abandoned when Mom refused to leave Dad. Absolutely no one was looking out for my welfare.*
>
> *My dad's brother offered to take me in. Uncle Nate knew a lot about my dad, probably more than I realized. Nate and his wife only had one child, a girl, who was six or seven years older than I was. I spent a lot of time over there. Uncle Nate was just trying to save me from a bad situation. It crushed me that Mom would not leave Dad. She had told me that the reason for her becoming an L.P.N. was so that she could afford to leave Dad.*

There is a cloud that hangs around my twelfth or thirteenth year, something more of the same or something different. There's a gap there in my memory that I can't fill in.

I know now that there were at least three incidents where I was tied up in my mom and dad's bedroom.

*   *   *

Chapter 7

Ron is here following yesterday's snowstorm. He doesn't remember much of the past few days; he's been dissociating. Barbara says he has been talking and not making any sense, like he's kind of incoherent. Ron tells me that a couple of nights ago he had an interesting memory. When he was around age eleven, his dad was taking Valium and drinking at the same time. Ron remembers that he used to crush up a couple of the Valium tablets and put them in Dad's beer. This would make his dad go to sleep and it would give Ron several hours of peace.

Ron remembers that around age nine, Dad started not hiding the fact that he was a drinker. He became very open about it with his beer, but kept secret his use of hard liquor. I ask Ron what kind of relationship he had with his sister, and he said "good." I suggest he give her a call and ask her if she remembers experiencing any kind of sexual abuse at the hands of Dad.

Ron is able to remember in detail the incident of punching his dad in the face and "knocking his lights out." Ron feels that there is something in the back of his mind that is nagging at him. He remembers untying his mom in the bedroom and his dad hitting him from behind. Ron kicked backwards and hit his dad in the shin. Ron then punched his dad in the face again. It turned out to be a slugging match and Mom made him stop when Dad was getting seriously hurt. Each day or two more details of Ron's memories are coming back. I ask Ron how it felt to hurt his father. Ron says he felt very good standing up to him.

Ron's dad worked for the railroad company department at a large chemical plant. He started out at the bottom and ended up as a general manager for the railroad. The railroad handled all types of sulfur and ore. Dad did well at the job and Ron remembers only one occasion when his dad missed work because of a hangover.

Ron was often embarrassed by his dad showing up drunk at his sandlot baseball games. Dad would yell from the stands for the entire game. He would yell at the umpire, the coach, or Ron himself.

His dad would also show up at his camping trips, making a nuisance of himself, often looking ragged and drunk. His drinking caused him to be far from coherent, and his appearance was a disaster.

One time Dad fell into a neighbor's front foyer, dead drunk. Ron was very embarrassed. Dad would give Ron permission to do something like visit a friend or go camping, but then on the following day, Dad would be very angry because Ron was going to be away from home. Ron basically gave up his social life to keep peace in the family.

Ron was active in community clubs, like one sponsored by the Rotary organization. He also took part in other community service activities with his peers. Ron belonged to the school yearbook staff, and had a top position in the organization. He belonged to the school band and to the speech club.

Dad was disappointed in Ron for not trying out for the school football team. Ron weighed only about 120 pounds, and instead chose the school band. At first, Ron played the trumpet, but later switched to the saxophone.

Because Dad did not like the noise level in the house when Ron was practicing, Ron was forced to go out into the woods to practice or stay after school. Even under these conditions, Ron thoroughly enjoyed the school band experience.

Ron has a distant memory. One night at age 13, while in his shelter behind the house, he observes his dad with a very large duffle bag or suitcase. His dad is emptying the contents and burying them. The next morning, with great curiosity, Ron follows a hunch and digs up the contents and discovers an entire woman's body in pieces. In later sessions Ron goes into detail about the discovery. At this point in time Ron is dissociating to age 12 or 13, unable to go into detail because he is so shaken up.

Barbara is not feeling too stable because in sessions with me Ron had been trying to change his story about watching his father burying the body parts. For some reason he is having difficulty processing this whole matter, possibly because he is thinking of his dad as a possible killer. The idea of his father perhaps being a murderer, I explain to Ron, has to set off a variety of confusing feelings in him. In his sessions when he is free-associating, he is distorting a number of details of his story as if to explain that perhaps he was wrong in saying that he discovered the body parts. It is a fact that he did, but he is confused over how to process the information.

Monday's session with Ron is an interesting one. We agree that he is totally blocked as he pursues the body parts situation, and his mind is stopping him from taking a further look at it, so we agree to stay away from that subject, for a time and just have him take his sessions wherever his mind leads them.

He also talks in very basic terms about asking my help in getting Barbara to break the ice with her cousin Ed, who seems to be holding a grudge against her and Ron. Ron is unable to dissociate today and go into the past, largely because the last time that he did, it was very traumatic for him to have memories that he never thought were possible.

Barbara is having a rough time on two fronts. Front number one is her job, where she is kind of on thin ice as she looks for new opportunities. On the home front, strange things have been going on with Ron ever since he recalled "the body parts incident." This has been hard on him and I figure that he is dissociating a lot, due to the fact that he has not shown up for the last half dozen group therapy sessions. He continues to come to his one-to-one sessions although he has had "car trouble" a couple of times. It is clear that he is really blocking at this point and clearly shaken up by his discovery. He will be here in a few minutes and we will see where his free-associating will take us. He is scared about something and I'm not sure what.

During Barbara's one-to-one today we discuss her anxiety and depression as a result of two things: one, her being heavily criticized at work and, two, her attempting to cope with her husband's Dissociative Identity Disorder. Barbara has an anxiety condition that goes all the way back to her days as a Ph.D. candidate at a major university. She eventually dropped out of the Ph.D. program, in part due to her anxiety and panic attacks occurring on a constant basis. She had no idea that the symptoms she was suffering were anxiety-related and thought they were related to her asthma, chronic bronchitis, and migraines. She only had a couple of chapters to finish writing on her dissertation and the final oral defense of that dissertation. She had an immense difficulty with exams and the anticipatory anxiety leading up to them. She carries with her constantly the feeling of failure for not completing her Ph.D. and of course I try to give her some emotional support over that situation. I remind her that there are plenty of professionals who suffer depression and are popping pills right and left, so having an advanced degree gives no immunity to emotional illness. She has taken a leave of absence with pay, and I urge her to take more time off, getting as much relaxation and sleep as possible prior to getting back to work. There are some procedures at work that she has to take part in that she feels incapable of handling. I think her feelings of inadequacy are not so much based on fact as on her anxiety condition. I plan to continue with Barbara in individual therapy and also in the women's group on Wednesday afternoons at 4:30. She is a very active participant in the group and is making a solid effort to get something out of it. She has some very intelligent and capable peers in that group, and she is getting and giving a considerable amount of help.

In Ron's session today, he states, "Dave, I'm going to introduce you to Ronnie at eleven years of age and maybe you can come to some conclusion." Barbara, Ron's wife, who is sitting in on this session says, "Eleven is the one sitting next to me with his head on my shoulder." Ron lies back and relaxes and switches to Ronnie eleven and says, "Hello, is this Dave? Can I call you Dave?" I reply, "Sure." Ron talks directly to Barbara while I am sitting in my chair and listening. Ron says, "Remember when I told you I was born with a double hernia? Well, I wasn't born with it. Dad tried to make me do things to him with my mouth and I refused. He would punch me in the stomach and toss me around the room. This one time I'm thinking of, I hit the corner of the dresser and the lower end of my stomach paid the price. I had to go to the hospital and Mom told me not to tell the doctor what had happened. I got badly hurt. Dad also tried at least once to put his thing in my butt, but it wouldn't work." I say to Ron, "Ron, I'm glad you can talk about what really happened. It takes great courage to remember this and be so open about it. I'm proud of you and I think everything is going to be all right, in time." Ron turns to Barbara and gets into a baby-like position and cuddles up to her as she pulls a blanket over him.

Ron has been having bad dreams in which either one of two splinters comes out. These are Ronnies age twelve and thirteen. In each case, Ron gets out of bed and gets next to Barbara in the form of Ronnie, and sitting on the floor, he kind of nestles a little bit next to Barbara to let her know that he needs some attention. Thirteen has told Barbara that he needs to talk about something that "Uncle Ron" (as the splinters call Ron), is not going to like. Ron says to me, "It's probably going to follow the same pattern as usual," meaning sex, as in sexual abuse. Ron wants to meet with me in Barbara's presence. He has asked this before when the sexual abuse came to consciousness. It is quite typical for him to ask for a session, saying that "something is pushing its way out." It seems like a planned dissociation. This is a very unique phenomenon in therapy. Ron cannot remember any trauma while conscious. He's completely blocked. He has to regress and dissociate in order for his mind to pick up what it is that's bothering him. And then, when the dissociation is over and he steps out of it, either Barbara or I interpret to him what just happened and then we begin to deal with it in therapy. Ron states, "Mother would never shut the door to her bedroom. A closed door meant either Mom wasn't in there or Mom and Dad were seeking privacy." I am not sure why Ron brings this subject up at this time other than to feel that the closed or open door is somehow related to the trauma that he is trying to remember. He feels certain, without my prompting, that there is more about the sexual abuse that has to come to consciousness. I don't want to plant any ideas in Ron, but I wonder, to myself, if the situations that may be trying to emerge involve Ron being a sexual slave to his father or his dad getting him involved with sexual acts with his mother. I'm very cautious not to suggest anything.

I just pick up on where Ron is headed, and he seems very obviously to be headed in certain directions. After quietly speaking in short sentences, He becomes tired. Barbara says to him, "It's OK, Ronnie. Just rest, Ronnie; I'll keep watch for you and keep you safe." I give Ron a chance to rest and then I interpret to him, when he ends his dissociation, that he didn't need to dissociate to remember what had happened in his childhood. I repeat to Ron what Eleven has said regarding more sexual abuse and I tell him that inherent in his needing to dissociate, is his judgment that he took part in doing terrible things. I tell him that he is a good person and that he was merely the victim of a very sick person and that he had judged himself harshly and wrongly, and that he will soon be able to integrate all of the little Ronnies together. He will then control his life and control his level of consciousness. We end the session with a great big sigh of relief on Ron's part as he has accomplished a very painful but satisfying new level of awareness and insight.

* * *

Chapter 8

In this morning's group session Ron explains what he's going through with the
dissociations and where he thinks he is headed. I assist Ron to talk about the
matter because I would like to get him to the point where he can really discover
what's going on in his head through regular therapy sessions, not needing to
dissociate to get some valuable information. Later, Ron and I discuss having his
wife Barbara present as we pursue this difficult set of memories, and we agree to
have some sessions without her attending to see if Ron will repress sensitive
subjects. However, we leave the door open to having Barbara return for some
sessions if this doesn't work out and we need her help keeping the little Ronnies
feeling safe (by sitting next to Ron and holding his hand or giving him a hug) so that
the memories can emerge.

Angie is interested in discussing Ron's dissociative behavior because several
months ago, she suffered similarly. She has not dissociated in several months, and

is very excited about her progress. She is also quite hopeful about Ron's progress. She speaks out, encouraging him quite a bit.

Today I remind Ron that he shouldn't just sit around and try to remember things. I tell him that he should concentrate on accomplishing household goals and begin thinking in the direction of doing some volunteer work, preparing for employment. I tell him that he will find the most certain way of not remembering stuff is to sit around trying to remember. Stuff will come back when and if he is ready, and we can't be sure that all repressed material will come to consciousness. We have to respect the wisdom of the mind and its protective tendencies. Perhaps some things never need to come to consciousness. There are times when we have to move on and deal with the present.

Ron remembers at age eleven building his shelter in the woods and often escaping from his dad and spending the night there. Today he is becoming extremely resentful of the fact that there was no one, including Mom, to observe what he was doing with himself and how his mental health was deteriorating. This insight is painful to him because it involves his sense of disappointment again in his mom while he was going through a period of severe depression. No one knew what was going on in his mind and it seemed like no one cared.

I'm working with Barbara to help her deal with Ron's DID and to fill me in on the pieces of Ron's dissociative behavior that she observes when they are together in

40

their apartment. This Monday morning Barbara explains the presence of one of

Ron's personalities called Shadow:

After several months, I thought that I had met all Ron's splinters up to age thirteen; then all of a sudden, I find out there's a "Fourteen." All the little ones thought that Fourteen was the angry one, and one day he came out briefly and said, "No, no, I'm not the angry one. I'm one that nobody sees much. I have to protect Uncle Ron. I'm holding the angry one back." I didn't understand who he was holding back and asked him what he meant. Fourteen said, "Well, there's a shadow person, and he's bad, and I have to hang on to him because he's the one who does the bad things." When I asked, "What do you mean?" he said, "He's the one who got on the computer and went to the bad places and he's the one who started ordering things." I'm thinking to myself, these "bad" things were subscriptions to porno internet sites, but a work from home pyramid business had also been started, so I was really confused. I replied, "But Nine told me that he's the one who started the Internet business." Fourteen said, "Yeah, Nine started it, but then he didn't know what to do with it, so he didn't do anything. I've been so afraid I'm the angry one, but there's the shadow one, so I don't know."

Out of the blue a couple of weeks ago, this one little part of Ron appeared. I didn't recognize any of his mannerisms, and I asked, "Are you the one that other Ronnies are calling Shadow?" And he said, "Yeah," and started to twitch. I have to admit that I got a little bit afraid, because we've suspected that Shadow is the one who pushed my mom across the room after an argument; that incident led to us getting thrown out of her house. Shadow had only come out briefly and then went back in. When Ron came back to himself, he asked for something to write on and began quickly writing adjectives like angry, mad, scared, cold, sad, etc. At that time, we didn't know what to make of that list.

This sequence of events leading to the "pushing incident" relate to the fact that I'm an only child and my mom and I have always been very close. We were invited to live with my mom seven years earlier when Ron and I both became ill and lost our jobs in the Atlanta area. On one particular day I was out back vacuuming the swimming pool. A few days earlier, on a rainy day, some steps for our new hot tub had been delivered. The packing material boards were still sitting on the grass and we were going to move them when the rain stopped. My mom came out of the house and said, "I wanted those boards moved yesterday." I said, "I'm doing the pool right now. I'll get to them when I'm done." My mom has back trouble and I wanted to avoid having her make herself sore, but she thought that I was treating her "like an invalid" by telling her that either Ron or I would take care of them. Mom then announced that she would move the boards right then. I responded, "Well, look, just let Ron do it because he'll be able to move them just fine." I went in the house to get him, and I said, "Honey, Mommy wants to get rid of those boards, can you please do that?" Mom goes out and says, "I'm doing it! I'm doing it!" Then she went slamming back into the house and under her breath, but loud enough for Ron to hear, said, "I've got all these things to do, and this is ridiculous, I'm tired of being treated like an invalid by her." Ron got really upset and he said, "Don't talk like that." Then she said, "This is between me and my daughter." And he replied, "No, this is not between you and your daughter. This is between you and my wife." After that, the argument began in earnest.

She started yelling at Ron, and he started yelling back, and Mom said, "Well, I'm going shopping." Ron remained between her and the short steps leading down to the back door, and she said, "Just let me out of here." Ron replied that he didn't want to get into an argument. So Mom tried to push past him and leave the house. We have a short landing that is level with the kitchen and then two steps leading down to another small landing where to the right are steps that go to the cellar and to the left is the doorway that goes out to the porch. Mom wanted to get past Ron, and what we've pieced together is that Ron grabbed her shoulders to keep her from falling because she was moving so fast. She thought he was trying to do something terrible to her and started screaming and hollering, "Let go of me! Let go of me!" Ron said, "Fine," and then let go of her, aiming her towards the porch where she landed in her easy chair. I was out by the pool and couldn't hear much until she yelled "Let go of me!" and then started to cry. What we think now is that Shadow is the one was holding her back from the steps and then released her once there was no longer any danger of her falling down the cellar steps. They both stumbled down the two steps and Ron ended up with a huge bruise on his back, which slammed into the doorknob of the open porch door.

Mom screamed at me that she wanted that "no good, bastard" out of the house by the time she got back. She then left to go grocery shopping. I chased Ron around the house, grabbing all the car keys, trying to keep him from leaving and he just kept pushing past me. I stood in his way, he gave me a shove, and I landed on the floor. Then this nasty voice I had never heard before says, "I suppose you want me to pick you up. That's what's expected of me, and I'm not going to do that!" Ron then went running out of the house and up the street. I jumped in my car and went after him. I found him and got him calmed down a bit. He was going to leave me *because he said he was no good for me! I told him we'd go to a hotel. So we went into the bank and got some money, but all the hotels were full due to homecoming festivities for the University. The only place that I could think of to go was to a couple who we've bowled with for a number of years. We showed up on their doorstep and they took us in to talk. The husband said, "Look, Ron, everything's going to be fine." We told them what had happened and they managed to get Ron to lie down in their spare room and I went back to my mom's house to change clothes and then go to the hospital; my grandmother (my mom's mom) was in intensive care and I spent the rest of the day there. Ron didn't remember anything about that day at all when I asked him about it later. He had no idea how he managed to get to our friends' house.*

We ended up that day with my mother saying, "I don't want to see him in this house again. He is out and he's not coming back!" I replied, "Well, if he's not coming back, then I'm not coming back." All she could do was refer to Ron as my "no good goddamn stinking rotten bastard of a husband." Here my grandmother is dying in intensive care and Ron wants to come in to say goodbye to her, and my mother says, "Well, you're going to have to find some time when I'm not here because I don't ever want to see him again!" So the day before Nanny died, we managed to figure out a time when my mother wasn't going to be there and Ron got to say his goodbyes, too.

I surmise now that Shadow may be the aggressive one that occasionally came out after the time of Ron's car accident. If he didn't like what I was saying and I was standing in his way, he'd put his hands on my shoulders and firmly move me over by an inch and say, "I'm not talking about this now." He was nasty and bitchy and not my Ron!

Now Shadow seems to be coming out a bit more, and he's very confused. He doesn't know where he is or what year it is. Fourteen, who is the one who had been restraining him, came "tearing out" after Shadow disappeared into Ron and said, "See, I shouldn't have relaxed. I let him out!" Every once in a while I'm a little apprehensive about Shadow coming out. I don't want him to be the same one who would push someone or get extremely angry, but it seems like there's times when Ron will start saying, "I'm no good for you. I need to leave. I'm no good. I need to go to Atlanta. I'm doing terrible things. Your health is suffering. I need to get out." Then after a few minutes, Ron doesn't remember doing or saying anything aggressive. Such behavior seems to belong to Shadow.

* * *

Chapter 9

I am in the office now after a home visit with Sally who is doing well. While there, I receive a phone call from Barbara, Ron's wife, saying that Ron had lost his prescriptions, and has to be over at his psychiatrist's office at 8:30 A.M. in order to see him and get new prescriptions. She explains to me that Ron doesn't know how long the appointment will be and that he will miss his session with me today at 9:00 A.M. I explain curtly to Barbara that I do know his psychiatrist and he is just going to write out a prescription and take five or ten minutes, at the most, and Ron will be leaving his office, at the latest at 8:45 and his appointment with me is at 9:00. He can simply go directly from his psychiatrist's office to my office, and that he is to come no matter what time it is. It is urgent that I see him today, and I explain to Barbara that quite obviously Ron is confused about something or trying to hide something, and is trying to blow off his sessions with me and I will accept no excuses. He is to be in my office this morning, no matter how late he is. I explain to Barbara that he is obviously blocking something in his mind that he is fighting off, but whatever it is, it needs to come out; this is an urgent part of his therapy. She agrees, and she places a phone call to Ron explaining my message. I hang up and after talking with Sally and her husband for five or ten minutes, I give Barbara a call back and ask her if Ron got the message to be here, regardless of the time. She says yes, and I explain to her that I will let her know if he does not show up, but he absolutely needs to be here if he is to continue the progress that he has made. I am waiting at this moment; it is 9:00 A.M. and will continue to wait for Ron.

After quite a while, at the beginning of my next patient's session, Ron knocks on the door, knowing fully well that after the forty-five minutes that he missed, a new patient would be in the office. So he pokes his head in while I am with another patient and I ask him briefly, "Did you get to see Dr. Harmon?" Ron says yes and I ask him if he got any prescriptions and he says yes. At this point, I am responding to Barbara's urging, in her latest phone call, to make Ron show me his prescriptions. Doing thus, I ask and he says, "I already filled them; I just went to the pharmacy." So I say, "OK, I'll give you a call and we'll set up appointments."

At this point, I call Dr. Harmon and find out that not only did Ron not have an appointment with him this morning, and thus did not get any prescriptions, but he has not seen Ron in several months. He says that he had seen Barbara and Ron once several months ago, and that was the only time. He had instructed Ron not to come to appointments, because he simply had missed too many sessions and is not wanted as a patient any longer. Therefore, Ron had been lying to his wife and to me about getting his medication and also about his visits with Dr. Harmon. What a dilemma!

At this point I place a call to Barbara and I tell her that I absolutely want to see her and her husband this evening. I will stay an extra hour late on this Friday evening to clear up whatever the hell is going on. She agrees. At 5:00 P.M. Ron and Barbara come into the office and I explain that we have quite a situation, and I don't understand why Ron is avoiding his sessions since he has gotten so much out of them. He is confused as well, and states that this whole situation with the body parts is very painful and he is worried about what will come out of his mouth after this, so he's ambivalent about the sessions. I assure him that we can get past it, and he can talk about whatever is on his mind. We can continue to discuss anything, be it the gruesome situation we have been handling or anything else that he wants to talk about. If we need to move away from the body parts subject temporarily or permanently, that's fine, but I explain that avoiding therapy is certainly not going to help his mental health. At this point Barbara asks me if I had talked to Dr. Harmon today and I knowingly lie, for my own purposes, and I tell them that I was not able to get him on the phone. Then I ask Ron how his session went today with Dr. Harmon. He says "good," that he gets along very well with him. I ask Ron if during his sessions if he does anything much else besides monitoring medication, and he explains, yes that they talk quite a bit about several things involving Ron's case, in the fifteen minutes that he gives him. At this point, I tell Ron that he has been lying, that he has not seen Dr. Harmon in several months; as a matter of fact, he has seen

47

him only once and that was with Barbara. So the question of prescriptions lately is crucial as well as his dishonesty. At this point Barbara is looking at me and looking at Ron, totally perplexed, and she asks Ron why he has not been honest about the sessions with Dr. Harmon and the prescriptions. Ron responds that he does not know why he has been doing this and that he is extremely confused. We talk for a few minutes and still, with the backlog of very positive therapy sessions Ron and I have had, I am hopeful to figure out this psychological maze. We talk for a while, but nothing positive comes out of the confusion. At the end of the session I realize that Ron is in quite a dilemma; what he had to gain from lying about the sessions with Dr. Harmon, and the prescriptions as well, is absolutely nothing. Neither Barbara nor I can figure out why it was necessary to be dishonest and Ron apparently can't figure it out either. Upon leaving the session, I put my arms around Ron, recognizing his confusion, and I give him a big bear hug. That is obviously what he needs at this point. Moreover, I reassure him, and tell him, "Don't worry Ron, we've been very successful working together; we will figure out what is going on." Dissociative behavior, at times, gets out of control. Patients, at times, can find themselves hundreds of miles from home, days later and have no idea how they got there. Where to go from here? We shall see.

In my brief conversation with Dr. Harmon today, we consult with each other about Ron and he says to me, "Dave, you've got a lot more than a Dissociative Disorder there; you've got a psychopath." Wow! I appreciate Dr. Harmon's diagnosis, but we really need to have some evidence of the psychopathic tendencies since Ron has lived for forty-five years and has been married to Barbara for twenty-two years; if he were a psychopath, we would have some kind of data and observations over the years to show that, so I am still perplexed. I suppose it is possible that if Ron were a psychopath, he could be extremely good at sociopathic and/or psychopathic behavior, even to the point where Barbara does not know of some of his activities, but personally, I think that it is impossible that this kind of psycopathy would not leak out during a long, successful marriage.

Here, Ron explains the complete confusion regarding the missed appointments with his psychiatrist, and his dissociative behavior:

> *OK! Dr. Harmon is the psychiatrist that I had started to see for regulating my meds, and my memory tells me that I've seen Dr. Harmon four times now, including the introductory visit when my wife Barbara was present. I have a firm memory of the visits, but I found out Friday that I had not been seeing him, that I had not seen him at all following the initial visit. This is the reality of the situation, yet my reality says that I had been talking to him; I'm suffering from a lot of confusion trying to figure out what's real and what isn't. This one really shook me up. It caused me to have a lot of dissociations over the weekend after I found out about it, and it has really sent me into a tail spin, because it now seems that reality is not something that I can necessarily judge anymore. I'm going through a lot of confusion about what's real and what isn't. Apparently, there's some part of me that didn't want to see Dr. Harmon, but wanted everybody to think I did. None of this makes any sense to me, but it seems to be a common pattern ever since this whole thing started.*

In Ron's session today, we are trying to recapture the spirit of therapy that has been so productive, yet has been lost during the past week or so. Ron had been trying to deny and distort his verbiage regarding finding his father burying body parts of a

49

women. During this past week, he has had several dissociative episodes because of the pressure put on him.

Yesterday's and today's sessions with Ron prove to be extremely innocuous and it is clear, as he sits and free associates, that he is going to be leading us into something that is fairly important. Knowing him as well as I do, I can kind of see what happens before it takes place. Remember, he is remembering many things from his past for the first time.

* * *

Chapter 10

Today's session with Ron and his wife, Barbara, proves to be completely fascinating.

For the past several days, both Ron and his wife have been preparing me for today's

session. Ron has told me that he has something coming into his mind that might be

along the same lines as earlier memories, such as sexual abuse or violence. As a

result of Ron's level of tension over the matter, today he has his wife in on the

session with him. He really doesn't know what it is, but he knows it is heavy. He

starts out by remembering a scene of Mom and Dad talking in the bedroom and he's

outside the bedroom and cannot hear the conversation. At this point in his narration,

Ron is in a state of complete dissociation and is about twelve years old. He

remembers Dad tying Mom spread-eagled to the four poster bed. Dad is trying to

get Ron to undress and to get involved in sexual intercourse with his mother. Ron

refuses, saying that he will have none of this stuff. Dad is angry about Ron's refusal,

and one thing that Ron is startled by today as he recalls this situation, is the level of

his mother's cooperation in the endeavor (cooperation with his dad, that is). Until

now, he had thought of her more completely in the mother role, but in the sexual situation, she is fully cooperative with her husband and not fighting him off at all. As a matter of fact, she encourages Ron to just do as Dad says. Ron refuses the chance for sexual intercourse, but after pausing his narration for several moments, he remembers his father forcing him to perform oral sex on him. Up to this point, Ron has not been conscious of this sexual act, but he is recalling it now, and equally upsetting is his memory of his mother's active involvement in the situation. As we end the session, Ron eases up on his almost hypnotic state, and I go over what has just happened. We talk mostly about Mom's involvement in the whole mess. One of the reasons why Ron had repressed these sexual activities is that, by remembering them, Mom comes off her pedestal, and now he sees her as someone who perhaps had some sense of enjoyment in the encounters. Furthermore, he is in a state of shock that his mother would encourage his involvement in doing what Dad said, such as doing oral sex on him. Today's session is extra burdensome, and I tell Ron that I will see him in a few days for our next session.

Ron has given me fair warning that there is more that is trying to pop up into his mind that he isn't conscious of. He comes into the office today, Monday, with his wife Barbara (she has taken a two week leave of absence due to stress). He puts his head back on the rear portion of the loveseat with Barbara next to him, and he begins dissociating and talking. There's quite a bit of discussion about the rifle that Ron remembered as a potential threat during an earlier session. Mom tells Ron that he should go along with whatever Dad wants because Dad just got a new rifle. Ron is convinced that his father is perhaps going to shoot him or his mom or the both of

52

them. Ron has hidden the rifle; Dad wants it back. Dad brings Ron into the bedroom where his mother is tied up spread-eagled on the bed, and he proceeds to tie Ron up. In the meantime, Ron's mom is encouraging him to do just as his dad says. Ron does not like the tone of her voice because he doesn't size her up as being especially frightened. He's beginning to think more and more of her giving a sizeable level of cooperation to Dad in his exploits. Dad orders Ron to get up on the bed and begin having sex with his mother. He refuses once again, and says that he will never go along with that. In the meantime, Dad begins having sexual intercourse with Mom and has Ron in such a position so that Mom follows through with doing oral sex to Ron. One can see that he is in agony as he explains what is going on. They finish, and there is further discussion about Dad wanting the rifle back. Ron is afraid that Dad will shoot him, but Mom again encourages Ron to cooperate. Ron is astonished at the lack of fear in Mom's voice. As Ron speaks about these activities, it is apparent, from his voice and body language, that he is becoming quite upset and is astonished to believe that perhaps Mom is actually getting enjoyment out of this bizarre enterprise. Ron gets down off the bed, gets dressed, and goes to fetch the rifle for his father. His father stands in front of him and, with the butt end of the rifle, smashes Ron across the face, and then shoves it deep into his stomach. Dad then punches Ron in the face. At this point in the narrative, Ron takes deep breaths and seems to come to consciousness in an upset fashion. I recap for Ron what he has just related to Barbara and me, namely the sex acts between the three individuals; the violence of his father towards him; and the awareness in Ron that his mother is not at all motivated to leave her husband, or

53

even to protect Ron. In fact, Mom seems like a genuine partner in the whole mess with her husband. Now that Ron is in a conscious state, we discuss the situation and he is most upset about is his mother's role in the situation. Prior to today, Ron had thought that his mother had been too frightened of her husband to leave him and run away with Ron. But more and more, Ron is becoming aware that there might be more to the situation than meets the eye. Ron is gravely disappointed in his mother, whom he has thought to be his great protector. As of today, he has some new insight into her role in the disaster.

Ron feels that an important portion of his memory involves year thirteen. He feels that there has to be more to be remembered. He still is switching personalities during the daytime, becoming thirteen-year-old Ronnie. His preoccupation with his thirteenth year indicates he is repressing trauma from that year. At least this is his perception.

Ron has particular difficulty with his mom's broken promises. She had completed her L.P.N. training while leaving Ron alone with Dad. Even when Mom got her diploma, she was unable to take Ron and go out on her own. His mom's change of heart left Ron feeling very disappointed in her and extremely depressed about his living situation.

Ron goes over the incident of discovering his father burying something and the resultant discovery of the body parts. Today he reviews this in clear fashion in a similar way that he let this information out for the first time with me. In other words, no distortions, no denial, no lying about any of the process which I believe was meant to take me off the trail of his father and I explain this to Ron, and he agrees with me. It is possible, from listening to Ron, that his mother arranged to move the body parts to another location, probably a location that would not point the finger at either she or her husband as the culprits.

Ron will be in for his next session shortly and we will see where his insight takes us. In the meantime, he is performing well on his new full time job. However, he seems to have re-injured his neck on the job and the result may be a lot of physical therapy. This injury is connected with the automobile crash of a year and a half ago that, for some reason or other, resulted in the "shock treatment" that caused him to remember the abuse in his childhood. From that point on in his memory, he developed the Dissociative Identity Disorder, or as most people refer to it, Multiple Personality Disorder.

In Ron's session today he explains in further detail about what happened with his discovery of the body parts on his parent's property:

> *Down near the spring that supplied our home with water there's a large creek that flows by. And on a little triangle of land that lies next to the creek, at the spot where I saw my dad burying stuff, I began digging. I found a foot sticking up out of the ground out of what, I guess, would look*

like a shallow grave. It was a depression in the dirt. I was twelve or thirteen at the time, and on discovering the foot, I went up and told my mother about it at my first opportunity.

I ask Ron to explain some of the confusion that he had about this discovery as he recalled the details.

Yeah, there was the confusion earlier when I first remembered this. I saw my dad digging the hole, and then he put the contents of what to me at the time looked like a camper's bag into the hole. The earlier memory had me uncovering the body and actually moving it myself to another location, and also taking pictures and then showing the pictures to my dad to prove to him that I knew he had done this. And also taking some of the pictures aside and trying to find somebody to hold on to them so that I could hold it over Dad's head, so that he wouldn't hurt me any more. That particular memory turned out to be false. This one seems a lot more realistic and I'm a lot more comfortable with it. The only explanation I have is that the earlier recollection must have been my ego dealing with something that I still didn't want to deal with; namely, my mother, basically betraying me on my telling her about this. When I told her what I had found, at first, like I said, she really didn't believe me. I took her down and actually showed her the location and showed her the foot. At that time, she started crying, but she recovered fairly quickly, I thought, for what had been discovered, and told me that it was OK, that she would figure out what to do with it and told me not to worry about it. At the time, I took that as a parent telling a child, "It's OK. You did fine and we'll figure out what to do"; just basically taking the responsibility away from a child who shouldn't have it anyway. I cannot be positive what she did with the information. The only thing I know for sure is that after telling her and showing her, the very next day I went down again, and the body parts were gone. It was obvious that the hole had been re-dug and filled back in, and when I found Mother again after that and asked her about it, the gist of her answer was, "It needs to be our little secret; we took care of it." So I can't honestly say that I know for a hundred percent sure what happened. I assume the body parts were moved again to a different place. As far as I know, the authorities never found out about it, because I assume that I would have been questioned if they had been.

I ask Ron, "Do you still want the authorities involved after all these years?" He responds:

> *Yes, but the only thing is that I don't have anything to turn over to them any more because I never knew what happened to the woman. They could link that, I suppose, with a missing person of the time. It was a lady. I did uncover her face so I know roughly what she looked like. My gut tells me that it may have been a lady who lived in town and had a reputation for having men in her house. I guess you could call her the town prostitute. Remember, the place is real rural and real small, so I can only imagine that one or two prostitutes probably were plenty for the market at hand. I remember the missing woman's name as Lenora or Leonora and, although nothing was said directly to me, I do remember overhearing that this particular lady had been missing, basically just disappeared. According to Mom, at a later time, she let me know that Dad had been seeing her. He had a habit of getting all dressed up and going out on numerous Saturday nights. I guess a real frequent meeting place for them was a motel known as The Desert Sands that was owned and run by one of Dad's drinking buddies.*
>
> *Actually I'm not sure that the whole body was there, but I know that there were two legs, a foot, and of course her head. I never dug around enough to find out whether there was actually a torso there or not, because at that time that's when I went to tell Mother about it.*

After the session when Ron discussed the body part situation, he went home and talked to his wife Barbara about the whole thing. She told him that she remembers Ron's mom telling her about his dad going out on Saturday nights with someone having a name similar to Lenora or Leonora, and that coincidentally the local lady of the evening suddenly disappeared. This corroborates Ron's memories. Apparently Barbara and Ron's mom developed a very close relationship and at times Ron's mom would just start talking about things that happened when Ron was young. Some of those things she asked Barbara not to tell Ron, so that he wouldn't be embarrassed or hurt, but she did say that there may come a time when Barbara would need to tell Ron and that Barbara would know when that was.

Barbara is reporting on her leave of absence from work while she recovers from her anxiety and depression. The anxiety condition has been with her for many years, and she is petrified about either losing her job or coming under further heavy criticism. She reports that Ron's progress is great in therapy. She is seeing me in one-to-one therapy as well as being in the women's group. I tell her that I spoke to her company's insurance company and requested a one-month leave of absence for her from this date on. She is happy that I am cooperating with her.

*　　*　　*

Chapter 11

In today's session with Ron, he remembers an incident that is very startling and very painful. He and his dad get into an argument, and Ron picks up the .22 rifle and aims it at his dad. His dad verbally challenges him, saying, "Put that thing away, boy! You're going to hurt someone." Ron says to his father, "You'd be surprised what a person can do when they don't care if they live or die." Ron fires the .22 through a window and seems to scare his father a little bit. This is a brand new memory and is, of course, very upsetting to Ron because he was basically using a weapon to intimidate his father. The thought of this level of anger at a parent is very upsetting to him. However, this is the first time he did not feel the need to switch personalities and become Shadow, in order to be aggressive.

At the end of this session, we review the fact that Ron did not lose consciousness and dissociate. He was not talking in the first person; he was just sitting there, discussing what he remembered. This whole point about whether or not he is conscious when he goes back and relives something is an important point as far as the type of therapy that we are doing. It seems as if, as time goes by, and Ron gets more used to recalling these memories, he is dissociating less and less, and he is simply responding like any other patient in the office discussing his memories.

We have uncovered many memories with the aid of Ron's "splinters," so I ask Ron's wife Barbara to explain some of the different personalities and different ages that Ron gets into. In particular, she speaks about something that's fairly new to us in dealing with Ron's situation; that is, the concept of Shadow and how he relates to Ronnies Twelve, Thirteen, and Fourteen.

At this point in time, I mostly see only Eleven, who's really close to the surface, and he tells me how the other little ones are doing. I can always depend on him to let me know what "Uncle Ron" or "Big Ron," meaning Ron in the present (my husband), has done during the day. Ron can't get away with anything, like having a headache, being dizzy, or falling, you know, things like that, without Eleven telling me. Currently, the younger Ronnies (Seven, Eight, Nine, and Ten) are being very quiet because they sense that some "scary" and "sad" things are being talked about by the older ones. Twelve is always cold and frightened, so when he talks to me, his soft, warm Barbara, I often put a shawl or blanket over him. He particularly likes it when I cover him with what he calls the "momma blanket." This is an afghan that Ron's mom crocheted as a birthday present for me the first year that we were married, twenty-three years ago. Twelve talks about how he feels, things that recently happened, recently being the late 1960's, and situations that confuse him about our present lives, in particular, this being Vermont in 2003, rather than South Carolina in 1969. He tells me that he's helping Thirteen, who has had the most recent memory about his dad tying his mom up and Dad making Ron try to have sex with him.

Until a couple of weeks ago, Fourteen always stayed in the background. I'd only met him twice until the day before yesterday when he came out and asked, "Is it okay if I have a hug?" I said, "Of course, Sweetheart,

*everybody needs hugs." He also asked, "Do I have to tell people
everything?" to which I answered, "Not until you are ready to talk about
those things. You're a part of big Ron that keeps those things safe in your
memory until you feel that its time to talk about them and help big Ron
remember them. When you're ready to talk, you can. No one is going to
force you to talk before you are ready."*

*Then last night, Ron and I were just sitting on the couch watching T.V.
and he snuggled up and put an arm around my shoulder. I can usually
tell from any twitching or positioning if one of the little Ronnies is about to
come out and who it is that is emerging. That's not to say that Ron and I
don't snuggle together as adults who love each other more than life itself;
we do, but often, when something is bothering him or one of the "little
ones," being close and relaxing will set the mood where a little Ronnie
emerges to talk about something or get a hug. Anyway, I thought it was
Eleven who came out, but he said, "No, I'm Fourteen. I think there's
something going on, but I don't think I know what to do about it." So I
said, "Take your time and just relax and think about it. When you're
ready, you'll be able to talk about whatever is bothering you and things
will come out." He told me he was the protector of the one that the other
Ronnies call Ron's Shadow, that he was the one who kept Shadow from
coming out and possibly saying or doing something nasty. Right after
Fourteen got his hug, he relaxed a little and then started to twitch a bit
and then, quite unexpectedly, Shadow emerged. I said hello to him and
asked him, "Do you know how old you are?" He replied, "No." I asked,
"Well, what would you like me to call you?" I had a chuckle afterwards
because he said, "Just call me Ronnie Shithead. That's all I'm good for.
I'm not good for anything. Nobody says I can do anything right." He
twitched a bit and then went away suddenly; Fourteen came "rushing'
back," quite upset that he wasn't able to keep Shadow away from me.
Fourteen said, "See, I can't let my guard down for a moment and Shadow
rushes out! Are you OK?" Once I assured him that I was fine, he asked
again, "If I want a hug, I can have one?" And I replied, "Yes, Sweetheart,
you can. Anytime that we're sitting here and you're feeling scared or you
just want a hug, I'll hold you. That's all we have to do. You don't have to
talk. You don't have to talk until you're ready."*

A couple of weeks later, during Barbara's one-on-one session, I asked her to further

elaborate on the emergence of Shadow and it's effect on some of the other Ronnies:

This just happened a couple of weeks ago: Ron was very agitated about some things and feeling very down about something. One of the little ones, I think it was Twelve, said, "There's one that sneaks around, but we can't see him. We think of him as the Shadow." The next day, Eleven came out; he's the one who's closest to the surface, and I said, "Hi, sweetie, how're you doing?" I gave him a hug, and he just kind of snuggled for a few minutes. I said, "Can I ask you a question? What do you know about this one that everybody's calling the Shadow?" Eleven said, "He's the one that sneaks by us. We can't really see him, but we think he's the one that hides things, like when Ron got rid of your pills, Aunt Momma." I asked Eleven, "But you don't notice when he's around?" He replied, "No." Twelve and Thirteen both came out after Eleven and I asked both of them what they knew about Shadow. They both said, "Yeah, there's a shadow guy. There's a Shadow; and he thinks he's the devious one." So I asked, "Okay, can Fourteen or the Shadow talk to me?" And Twelve said, "Well, Fourteen is holding on to Shadow real tight." Unfortunately Ron had a horrible headache after this big encounter, because he gets headaches when he switches, so we let the subject go for a day or so.

When I spoke with Fourteen a couple days later, he said, "Okay, I'll come out. I just want to get a hug and stuff." And then he got really upset and all of a sudden he changed, and I could tell from the slumping and the difference in Ron's posture that Fourteen wasn't there anymore and that this person we've been calling the Shadow was there again.

Shadow was really confused; he looked around and he didn't know where he was. I asked him, "How old are you, Honey?" He said, "I don't know." I asked, "What's your name?" He said, "I guess I'm Ron or Ronnie." I told him that we call the other Ronnies by number, according to age, and asked again what should I call him. He said, "You can call me Shithead." I said, laughing, "No, no, no, I'm not going to call you that." I reached over and put my hand on his shoulder and asked, "Honey, can I put my hand on your shoulder?" He said, "I didn't think you'd want to do that because I think I'm the one that does the bad things. I think I'm the one that sneaks around." And I said, "But you're all a part of big Ron. You're all little Ronnies. Just relax. You don't have to talk. If you want a hug, that's fine." He just kept saying how confused he was; he kept saying it was the seventies. Fourteen came zipping back out for a few moments and he said, "See, I told you! I can't let him out of my sight! I have to hold on to him!"

A few days later, I talked to Eleven, Twelve and Thirteen and said, "Fourteen needs some help with Shadow. He thinks he's the only one who can help." So Eleven, Twelve and Thirteen said they'd try to communicate with Shadow. Yesterday, Fourteen did come out, and we spoke for a little bit; he feels a lot more secure because the other ones are helping him, but he still feels really, really bad. There was one other time that Shadow came out and he said, "I don't understand where I am." I asked if he knew who I was, and he said, "I know that you're somebody very important to me." I asked if he knew my name, and he said, "Yeah, you're Barbara." Then he asked, "When is this?" and I told him it was 2003 and asked when he thought it was. He replied, "The seventies – and we have to be careful because Daddy's still around. We have to be careful." I told him, "Sweetheart, your daddy died a long time ago, and he's never going to hurt you again. You're in the process of remembering this stuff, so if you get scared, try to watch it like it's a movie on T.V. or something that you can step back from, and maybe that will help you to remember and not be frightened. Just remember that I'm here for you and all the Ronnies, and that I love big Ron and all of you very, very much. If you want to talk, fine. If you're not ready to talk or if Fourteen or anyone else isn't ready to talk, nobody has to talk about this stuff until they're ready. You know that you've always got me here to love you, you've got Dave, and Dave's a good man, so that's what you need to do. Whenever you're ready, you can talk. And if all you want is a hug, then you can have a hug." A sort of combination of Shadow and Fourteen then said, "I never had anyone to give me a hug just like that, for nothing." Then they just kind of faded away, and Ron fell asleep."

Barbara continued speaking about the personalities and the order in which she "met" them:

The first one that I met was Nine. Ron and I were staying in a motel after we had been kicked out of my mom's house after an "incident." All of a sudden, Ron sat forward on his chair, gazed around and asked "Where are we?" Not understanding what was going on, I asked, "Where do you think you are?" to which he replied, "We're in a waiting room; the doctors want to send me to another hospital. They don't know what my face is going to look like." He told me that his dad had been drunk and asked him to help "jump start" a car to recharge a dead battery, but Dad had the cables crossed and when he had Ron attach the last clip, the battery blew up and Ron's face, chest, shoulders, and arms were badly burnt. This incident occurred during the spring around the date of Ron's birthday, so both Nine and Ten have these memories. Nine does remember having to keep food hidden in his closet, because his dad often wouldn't let him eat. He also remembers hiding under the house because his dad hit him in the face. On a happier note, Nine likes to play with balls, has a comic book collection that Dad wants him to get rid of, and he loves hamburgers and french fries.

The next Ronnie that I met was Ten; he had bandaged eyes when he first emerged because of the car battery explosion. At one point, when his bandages needed changing and he and his puppy needed something to eat, he stumbled in on his mom and dad when they were having sexual relations and his dad tied him to the bed so that he could "watch." Ten loved to listen to baseball on the radio and cuddle and play with his puppy while his eye's were bandaged because of the battery explosion. This precious puppy was later killed by another dog when she crawled under the house to sleep with the other dog, who had just had puppies and was very protective of them. Ten heard noises under the house and crawled under it to try and rescue his puppy, but little "Princess" died in Ten's arms. Dad wouldn't let Princess sleep in the house with Ron on that particular evening; Dad had no sympathy for Ronnie Ten's loss of his "best friend."

Seven was the next "splinter" that I met. He is so curious and fascinated about everything; if you could bottle up his happiness and sell it, you'd be a millionaire! He has a big smile, and he doesn't just come out; he rushes out in a flurry, like the day that he found a kite down in our cellar and he tore through the living room, saying, "I found a kite! I found a, kite! Can we fly it?" When he first starts talking, it's not, "Hello" it's "We went on a picnic, Hi!. We had hot dogs and hamburgers and we played baseball!" He always talks about fun stuff, but occasionally some of the fun things are those that happened later on in Ron's life, so perhaps he holds in his memory the innocent and happy moments. The neat thing, the fun thing about him is that he's always smiling. We go outside and we blow soap bubbles together and he just loves it; he runs up and down the lawn just like a little kid. But the one thing that's rough with him is that he put his daddy on a pedestal. He loved his daddy; the one who used to take seven-year-old Ron to the freight yard at the chemical company and let him ride on one of the trains. Dad let him get up in a locomotive. Ronnie Seven followed Daddy everywhere, but seven was also the age when Ron first discovered that his daddy got drunk and Seven didn't understand; he thought Daddy was sick. Seven loved to play with dogs and play "rolly bat"; he can't understand why all the older Ronnies say mean things about Daddy because Seven's dad was a nice man; Seven remembers the fun and nice things about his dad.

Eight loves kites and doesn't think that he comes to see me; he thanks me for coming to see him. I first met him when we moved into our apartment. when I walked into the living room with a load of our belongings I spotted Ron sitting on my large steamer trunk swinging his feet back and forth *holding one of my stuffed turtles. He greeted me with "Hi Aunt Barbara; I knew you were here somewhere because Fuzzy is here!" This particular stuffed turtle that I'd named Fuzzy became the trigger that I could use to try and bring Ron back to the present if he had a flashback to a particularly difficult memory. I'd been taking Fuzzy to work with me so that if Ron dissociated while I was away from the apartment, he would know that if Fuzzy wasn't there, then I wasn't either. One of Eight's traumatic memories was having to sneak through a closet into his parents' bedroom where his father had tried to shoot himself by rigged up shotguns with strings. Because at eight-years-old Ron was the smallest member of the family, he was the only one who could crawl through the closet and try to see the arrangement of guns and strings. At eight years of age, Ron had to clip the string on the opposite door of the closet and grab it so that a gun wouldn't go off and cause his father to be shot. This wasn't the only time that Ron was exposed to his father's bizarre suicide attempts.*

Ronnie Eleven is the one closest to the surface. He seems to be almost like the normal Ron. He's very perceptive. Eleven tries to take care of everyone. He can almost always be relied upon to tell me what "Uncle Ron" has been doing, unless he has been intentionally blocked by one of the others. When Ron was eleven, he spent a great deal of time in a homemade shelter that he constructed in the woods. Eleven has a smile that lights up the room! He wants to protect everybody and greatly assisted Ronnie Twelve and Ronnie Thirteen when they were in the process of emerging.

Ronnie Twelve came out in a very sad way, always being cold and scared. When he first emerged, all he could do was say single words or short phrases, but gradually, over the last few months, he has started to talk in full sentences. I first met Twelve when he was cowering in a corner in our apartment, reliving the episode in the root cellar when he was in there with the bugs and the snakes. Twelve calls me "Soft, Warm Barbara." He is always cold and likes to be covered with a blanket. His father shut him in the root cellar or locked him in the spring house numerous times. Among other things, his father made him dig ditches in the middle of the night and clean already clean items. Twelve hid in the woods as much as he could. When he gives me a hug, he nuzzles against my neck.

Ronnie Thirteen is very, very scared; he was the one who actually attempted to slit his wrists while hiding out in his little shelter. Despite all the horrible things that he survived, often by spending lots of time in the woods, he gives the best hugs in the world! He always wants to be safe and calls me "Safe Barbara." Twelve and Thirteen often emerge together and call me "Safe, Warm Barbara."

It's really fascinating to watch the interaction of the older Ronnies. Eleven often helps Twelve to bring his memories forward during therapy sessions and Twelve helps Thirteen the same way; it looks like Twelve and Thirteen have helped to bring Fourteen forward. All of the Ronnies are bright. They're all loving. They all worry about me when something is bothering me, like a backache or headache. They sit down next to the bed and take turns making sure that I'm still okay. Consequently, Ron doesn't get much sleep on those nights.

To protect all of the little Ronnies and regulate Ron's medication, I keep Ron's and my medication bottles in a locked box and either wear the key around my neck on a chain or bury it in my purse, but a couple of times someone has taken the key, dumped some of the pills out, and then discarded them down the drain or down the toilet. We've come to realize that when medication is missing, it's because their father abused Valium, and Ron used to discard his dad's Valium so that he wouldn't be taking the Valium and drinking alcohol at the same time. The most recent time that medication was missing, they all said, "No, we didn't do it." Come to find out, it was actually Shadow who managed to do it. Shadow is the one who is always in the background; Fourteen seems to have taken upon himself the task of protecting everyone else from Shadow, but because he's been doing it alone, Shadow does manage to "slip by him" at times and did get into the medication box. Shortly thereafter, when Ron and I were sitting on the couch watching T.V., Ron started twitching his face, shoulders, and arms, and then Shadow emerged. He looked absolutely terrified and cowered a bit trying to look smaller than his size. I put my hand on his shoulder and asked him if it was okay if I put my arm around his shoulders and just talk to him. He said he didn't think I'd want to do that and stated, "I think I'm the devious one. I think I'm the one who's causing all this trouble. I don't understand where I am." He looked around and he didn't have a clue. Fourteen came out and said, "See, see, I let my guard down and he got out! Are you okay? Did he hurt you?" And then a few days after that when Fourteen came out again, I said I'd like to be able to help Shadow if and when Shadow was ready for it. Fourteen replied, "I don't know about that, but Eleven, Twelve and Thirteen are helping me take care of him now, so we'll be better able to keep a watch out for you and keep you safe." In the course of only a few more weeks, Shadow has emerged more frequently and has become very protective of me. I know when he is ready to come out because of his characteristic twitching and also that we hold hands with him cupping his fingers around mine almost like making a chain link. He is the splinter who has been around the longest and he remembers the last dog that Ron had in his life while living at home. This feisty half-dachshund/half-Chihuahua named Peanut was very special to both Ron and me. Shadow also remembers when Ron and I started dating when we were at the University of Georgia; at first, Shadow wasn't too thrilled at our developing relationship, but eventually he got used to the idea and now he's okay with it, thank goodness. He worries about me all the time because I suffer from severe, chronic back pain that is pretty much constant, so the first thing that he says when he comes out is "Barbara Mom okay?" We know that there will probably be bumps in the road as therapy continues, but Shadow is developing into a very sweet, kind, young man.

I thank Barbara for elaborating on the characteristics of Ron's "splinters" and I'm sure that as time passes she will be able to describe the changes that occur in Ron and the Ronnies as more memories emerge and the process of integration of the "personalities" into one "whole" Ron occurs. It may be that Shadow represents Ron's first dissociation, or at least one of the most important dissociations in his childhood. It's clear that Shadow is a very important part of this whole picture. Ron, at age fourteen, is a young man; he's much more assertive and aggressive with his father; he stands right up in his face and gives it right back to him whenever his dad is verbally abusive with his constant putdowns. Fourteen is a key here to this whole process.

*   *   *

Chapter 12

Barbara is still on her leave of absence from work and is doing pretty well being away from the job. Her stress load is diminished, and she is finding that her husband Ron is there for her in time of need as she was for him. They have a wonderful relationship.

Today's session with Ron explains Shadow and the other splinters in a much more meaningful way. Some of the difficulties that Ron had gotten into (in the months before his illness was recognized and diagnosed) when he started dissociating were basically legal difficulties. He would get on the Internet and would enter into tiered businesses in an attempt to make money, but Ron was not aware that these businesses had been started. A short time ago, Nine told Barbara that he started a business because it sounded like he could make some money for Ron, but then he didn't know what to do next. Ron was not consciously aware that these businesses had been started. Apparently, Shadow would get involved in pornography as well,

69

because Ron was receiving numerous E-mails of this type and didn't know how he'd gotten on these types of mailing lists. Shadow also signed up for subscriptions to pornographic web sites without Ron's knowledge. Today Ron talks in a dissociative manner and assumes the role of Shadow as he explains how he always tries to get people into trouble. This side of Ron is the aggressive, hostile, devious, undermining side of Ron. Even when Ron was in college, Shadow would come out and suggest to Ron that it was not necessary to write a term paper; it was not necessary for him to study for his next test, etc. He was always getting Ron into some kind of difficulty. Ron either thought that he had finished a term paper or some other type of assignment or didn't know that there was a test or quiz until he was seated in a class and the exam was being passed out.

Apparently, Ron has not been able to accept the part of himself that is a part of all of us, namely, the more impulsive, devious, and angry parts of ourselves. I explain to Ron that what we need to do is to allow him as Ron, not Shadow, to express some of the negative and hostile feelings that he has, understanding that we can work through those feelings. He does not need to dissociate to do this. If he can talk out these feelings, chances are he can set some reasonable limits on them, but when he dissociates and becomes Shadow, he does not know anything about limits. As a matter of fact, with setting up the internet businesses, Ron could have gotten himself into very serious legal trouble. Instead, he only got himself and his wife into trouble financially. Ron and Barbara are still working on cleaning up the debt that came from his adventures.

Ron does not have any difficulty accepting the fact that he can have a bad side of him, just like all of us, but this acceptance has only come through therapy. Apparently, over the years, he has never allowed himself to accept the fact that he could do some things that are very antisocial. Through therapy, we can keep a lid on things without forcing him to repress the kind of feelings that cause him to dissociate.

Barbara is completing her third week of short-term disability, and she has been enjoying the time she has gotten to spend with her husband Ron. She had a rough weekend, just anticipating the fact that she would be beginning work in another two weeks or so. She is very shaky and petrified of the idea of returning to her position as a trainer and technical writer, where she was severely criticized for a poor performance a few weeks ago.

It is obvious that she is building up a kind of phobia about returning to work, so I suggest to her that we take part in a little desensitization and not avoid reviewing her work, out of fear. I suggest she spend fifteen minutes a day for the next two or three days exposing herself to her homework for the job. I tell her that if she avoids it completely, the fear will just get bigger, but that she should just do a little at a time and start today with no more than fifteen minutes. I think this will get her over the hump.

During Ron's one-on-one today, he does not dissociate within the session; as a matter of fact, he is finding the dissociations more and more infrequent and, for once, he feels comfortable in going out into the community because he knows he will not "black out." He still is much more disappointed in his mother than in his father. All the time he knew his father, he knew exactly where his father was coming from, and his father's abuse of him accounts for a large part of his mental illness. But in the case of his mother, he had great expectations when she had promised that the two of them would move away from Dad, but she never fulfilled her promise. He continues to be very hurt by this because, at least with his mother, he did have her up on a pedestal, and now he is adjusting to her being without one.

The session today is not a very dynamic one, but there is certainly a great deal of satisfaction in Ron's mind, and in mine, that the drama is no longer very extreme. He has been offered a part-time job at the bowling alley as a maintenance mechanic (his area of expertise), and this is going to be his first step towards bringing home a paycheck, so he is excited and looking forward to beginning the position. However, he is walking around with an image of an axe falling on his head; he has had such bad luck while he has been going through the past several months, that he is anticipating trouble at every turn. He asks me why he is doing this, and my reply is that, if you go over everything since the car accident of fourteen months ago, there's been nothing but bad things that have happened, and at this point in his life his norm is for bad things to happen continuously, so he is just accepting that further crap will fall on his head. I remind him that he is going through a period of relative peace

72

right now and sure, he'll have his ups and downs, but there's no reason to assume that the guillotine will drop. Now he's busy getting used to the fact that maybe some decent things can happen to him and his wife Barbara.

Ron is wondering if his very direct treatment of George in the last group is the reason why George is not attending group therapy today. I tell Ron that's not the reason, and reassure him that he was not unfair at all to George in group. I do say that I wonder how George fits into the current group, since he is the only one who is actively psychotic. I do not have other actively psychotic patients that I can form a separate group with, so I ask this group to be tolerant of George, but to be very focused on how to keep him in check with reality.

Over the weekend, there was a major disappointment for Ron. He had told his wife Barbara, while she was working, that there apparently was some kind of a sewer pipe leak, and the apartment smelled like sewage. He had to get the situation cleaned up. When Barbara returned from work, there were no odors, but Ron indicated that it took quite a bit of effort and some particular kinds of chemical bombs in the apartment to clear up the odors from the outdoor sewage break. Ron had presented this in such a matter-of-fact manner that, although Barbara could not detect the odor of either sewage or chemicals, she believed that the sewage leak had really occurred. However, as circumstances unfolded, it became clear to her that there had not been a sewage leak; in other words, Ron had dissociated again and did some type of regression in which he felt he had smelled the sewage leak.

Subsequently, in our next session, it became clear that the dissociation meant that something needed to come out, so we attempted to gently pull it out. We didn't get too far, but Ron did make a point of telling us about an area deep past his house and past the old septic system and the creek. All I can make out of this situation is the sewage connection, and also the water connection, that is very active in Ron's dreams and in his dissociations. He has always wondered why he has this theme of water that reoccurs, but we have yet to put it together.

All this is going on while Barbara is returning to work after her leave of absence. She is there on a part-time basis, and it is clear that her company is making moves to either let her go or change her position drastically. She is incredibly upset and has to prepare in a day or so to teach a very technical class that she feels she could not possibly be expected to do since it is out of her area, but she is being told to do it and just do the best she can. She is toying with the idea of leaving the job immediately or putting forth 150% effort in teaching the class. She has decided to go ahead with the class, but while she is pursuing other job opportunities. We may have to extend her leave of absence due to the pressure the company is putting on her. They know that she has been out of work for emotional reasons, but they still continue to dump tasks on her that are very difficult. They are not giving her any time to adjust to being back at work. There's a lot of innuendo also that part of what they're doing is a pressure tactic, to hire a younger person to work at half the salary. This is all going on for Barbara while Ron has had the unexpected dissociation. However, Ron is back to work, nearly on a full-time basis in his area of expertise.

This has been something that he has done for years: doing repairs and tune-ups on the automatic equipment in bowling centers. He is doing quite well at work and so it seems like we cannot get Ron and Barbara fully functioning at the same time. We will see what happens, but generally speaking, there are a lot of good things happening as well as negatives. I react to Ron's dissociation as something good, because as usual, he is throwing up a warning signal that something is bothering him on an unconscious level. I try to interpret the latest dissociation to Barbara and Ron as something that, in a way, we could feel good about; it means we can uncover more that is deep behind Ron's conscious mind. It is very helpful that he is asking, through his dissociative behavior, for help getting out repressed material.

*   *   *

Chapter 13

Barbara is having quite a bit of difficulty in her first month back at her job. Her depression was significant and led to a leave of absence, but now she's back on the firing line. There are more unspoken hints from her company superiors that it might be better for her to look for a job elsewhere, which is what she's trying to do while still working at her present job.

Barbara feels she is doing better at work. The combination of therapy and medication has her somewhat stabilized. She is coping much better with Ron's difficulties. Barbara has found that doing things like swimming laps and playing racquetball is extremely helpful to her mental health, so she continues to do one or the other on a daily basis, and it is making a huge difference. She is trying to get her self confidence back, and is attempting to prove to her superiors that she is very capable of handling her workload.

Tonight's women's group is very small; people are away doing other things. Barbara is the main topic of concern this evening. Today she was suddenly fired from her job; she was escorted to a small room, told she was fired and would not be allowed to return to her desk to retrieve her personal belongings; they would be packed into boxes for her and taken to her car. This is the way that large corporations dismiss someone. They told her it was due to her lack of organizational abilities, but it is clear that they had been planning this for several months when one looks back at their actions. Barbara gets a good deal of support from her peers, and we talk about the benefits of not working for that company since she has been for quite some time uncomfortable with some of the tasks she had been assigned. I remind her that at this point, she can start over and look for a job with the functions that she is excellent at. The group gives Barbara a lot of support and encouragement. She is very frustrated, feeling that the past twenty-five years have been so full of ups and downs in her personal life that she is just worn out because of the "rollercoaster ride."

Ron's last three sessions seem very innocuous as he drifts back into the past and recalls his childhood. At this point he is discussing a lot of his hanging out in back wooded areas of his property, especially one area near the cemetery. At this point he is back there with his older brother. Apparently they did a lot of hanging out in the old cemetery. I do not know, at this point, if there is meaning to the issue of unmarked graves back there, but something is up regarding death. I do conclude, however, that it is possible that his father was a serial killer. This sounds grandiose and dramatic, but the question before me is why his father would have chopped his victim up into body parts. It seems to me that it is just as easy to carry a body to a wooded area and bury the body, whether or not it is in parts. It makes no sense, unless there is some very sadistic element of psychopathy within his father. I mention that often it is the case with serial killers who are very sick psychopaths, that they will do something to the body before burying it, such as slicing a woman from the jugular down to the vaginal area. I do not understand, nor does Ron, the necessity of chopping up a victim after killing her. At this point, Ron's sessions seem to be merely bridges to more important memories that will, hopefully, come out later.

We have had a turn of events regarding Ron's situation that is most startling. Previously I had discussed the matter with Ron about his father possibly being a serial killer just because I didn't understand the purpose that his father had in chopping the body of the woman to bits before burying it. It just didn't make any sense. If he was involved with the supposed hooker, and let's say she was trying to blackmail him or something, one can understand that a bad character like him might kill the woman to protect his relationship with his wife. But the business of cutting her into parts before burying her is certainly meaningful clinically.

In the following session it becomes clear that Ron's nervousness and brief dissociations had been taking place for a reason. Today Ron recalls the ravine that lies about half a mile to the rear of his house that was right next to what he refers to as the CCC road. This road was built during the earlier part of the 20th century during the Great Depression when the Civilian Conservation Corps (CCC) was active. I believe it featured activities for men who were not in military service, but needed to earn a paycheck. This was the time of the country's most severe financial crisis and the government had set up this program to basically keep food in men's bellies, and also keep them out of trouble with the law, while involving them in some sort of productive activity. At any rate, Ron recalls that one day he and his friend Kerry were fooling around near the ravine. In certain parts of the ravine it was as deep as sixty or seventy feet, while in other parts it was maybe only five or ten feet deep and this ravine stretched for a good distance, maybe a quarter of a mile or so. Ron (while dissociating) recalls that one day, getting close to the edge of the ditch, he sees a four-door Plymouth that looks just like a car his father had owned just a year or so ago. He swears this is his father's car. He and Kerry jump down where the ravine is not too steep and they go fishing around for whatever, being just two nine- or ten-year-old boys in search of adventure. Darkness falls and they have to go home, but Ron decides that he will go back at a time when Kerry is not with him, because he senses that there is something strange about the whole deal. A couple of days later he goes back. He looks in the car and does not see anything peculiar. Then he opens the trunk and he sees an axe and a knife, and both are covered with blood stains. He doesn't know what to make of the situation. Remember, this is a few years before his discovery of the buried body parts. Ron digs around further in front and in back of the car, and about fifty feet towards the rear of the car he spots a mound of earth that looks very much like somebody had been digging there. He uses some sharp long sticks and manages to do some digging and he discovers a women's foot (this one is not detached from the body). The woman is apparently wearing high heeled shoes. He is horrified and covers it up quickly. He heads back home wondering about the connection between his father's car, the bloody knife and axe, and the grave.

It becomes clear to me that I can pretty well predict when Ron is about to make some kind of important discovery in his own mind, by the number of dissociations he is having just prior to discussing these issues in therapy. I also suggest to Ron that it's going to be much more constructive to let out some feelings in a therapy session than to find himself dissociating on a highway, not knowing where he's headed or perhaps who he is. So I want him to, whenever he has any kind of inkling of any kinds of feelings coming into consciousness, keep a notebook and immediately write things down or else talk to his wife, Barbara, or else call me for a therapy session and I will juggle my schedule in an effort to see him.

Ron does recall talking to his mother about the old Plymouth that is in the ravine. He thinks he remembers bringing her to see the Plymouth. Ron does not understand why the car disappeared. Just to check things out, Ron and his mom go to the service station where his dad was supposed to have traded in the Plymouth to get his current car. Ron's mom is confused because her husband told her that the Plymouth was used as the down payment. They talk to the garage owner and the garage owner explains that he never saw the Plymouth, and there was no car used as a down payment. Ron's dad had lied to her or deceived her in some way; she is sure of this. Why would he lie about the Plymouth as a down payment? At this point, the session ends and we will pick up in a few days.

Chapter 14

Barbara is in for her one-on-one and wants to explain some of the dissociations that Ron is having at home:

OK, pretty much it's kind of interesting, for a while, food was no problem, but now we had another incident last week where Ron ate a whole bunch of mom's yogurt that was in the refrigerator, and he doesn't remember doing it. (Ron's dissociations involving food have to do with the fact that his dad would punish him by not allowing him to eat for days at a time.) So I asked him about it and he said, "Gee, I'll have to think, I don't remember doing it." Then he said to me a few hours later, "I think that the kids are a little bit upset, either upset or scared or angry, and one of them did the eating because he was afraid that you were mad at them." It sounded like "the kids" and I needed to talk, so I went ahead and suggested that we go into the living room together and sit in the double recliner. I asked Ron put his head on my shoulder, and I put my arm around his neck and shoulder and asked him to just relax.

Once he was relaxed, I just said, "So, does somebody think I'm mad at them?" and little Thirteen came out and gave me a hug and said, "Well, we were worried cause you fell asleep the other night so fast and we didn't get a chance to give you a hug." Then Twelve came out and said, "Everything OK Aunt Barbara? You hurt?" and then Eleven came out and said, "Yeah, I think that Shadow is still unsure, but he may be the one that did the eating." So I said, "OK, guys" and I was just quiet for a few moments and held onto Ron real tight and kind of rubbed his arm and then I asked, "Is my Shadow in there? Shadow, are you there? Would you like to talk?" and I could feel twitching; there's a particular kind of twitching that Ron does when Shadow is the one that's coming forward, and he only dissociates now pretty much with me, and little Shadow came out and just was hugging me real tight. He always does that; I know it's him because of the way he holds my hand. And then he does the "I love you" sign that the deaf use [this is American Sign Language, or ASL, which Ron learned some of in high school and took courses in when he was in college] and he puts it on my heart so I know it's him. So I asked him what the problem was and he said, "Well, we were all gonna cuddle, and I was going to get a hug and you fell asleep too fast, and I thought you were mad at me, so I thought that I better make sure that I had plenty of food." And I told him, "Sweetheart, you know I love you, I love Uncle Ron, I never lie to you, I'm never going to lie to Uncle Ron and everything is fine. I just have a lot of pain in my back right now, and I took some medicine, and it made me a little bit sleepy, and that's why I fell asleep so fast." So he said, "It's OK?" and I said, "Yes, honey, it's fine." Then I said, "You know that any time you get scared that you can let us know, and you know that there's always going to be food in the refrigerator. You don't have to hide it. You don't have to sneak it. You don't have to stock up and eat a whole bunch, because what you're doing is eating a lot of extra food and you could make Uncle Ron feel sick and then you all are going to feel sick and we don't want that." So, Shadow seemed to understand and I just held him for a little while and then I said to him, "You know, everyone else calls me Aunt Barbara or Momma Barbara; Eleven calls me Aunt Momma, but you don't really call me anything. Would you like to figure out what sounds good to call me, whatever makes you feel comfortable?" And so he said OK, and then last night, when Ron and I returned home from our bowling league, we sat in the chair for a little while and Shadow came out of nowhere and all he said to me was, "love Barbara. Barbara love." and then he said, "Barbara Mom!" So I have a feeling that he's going to call me Barbara Mom. Shadow is very, very fragile, very timid; he thinks that he caused all the problems that Ron had all through college, and in a way he did, because he was the one that wanted Ron to not study, and he played tricks on Ron. However, I think that we are turning the corner now, that little Ron, little Shadow Ron, has finally decided that he's going to start to interact a little bit more. He says he can now see through Uncle Ron's eyes a little bit and the other Ronnies are all starting to help him. So, I think that's a great sign. All of the Ronnies are just so tender and sweet and it seems like all they want to do is have hugs, and so that's what we do. I make sure at night that everybody gets a hug if they want it. I don't pull them out, but if my husband, Ron, gets nice and comfy and we're just watching TV, one of them might just kind of pop out and give me a little *hug and say, "Good night Aunt Barbara!" So, you know, that's kind of neat. We're coming along. There's a few things that Shadow says he needs to talk about with Dave and there's a few things that Thirteen still needs to talk about with Dave, but I think we're doing well. So, that's kind of a summary of the way this happens.*

I was a little afraid about Shadow a few months ago because I didn't know what to expect, but now he's just like the way Twelve was when he first came out and was very scared and needed to be held. Now Twelve does the holding, gives the hugs. That's the same way with Thirteen; he needed to be held, but if Ron sees that I need a hug and Ron gives me a hug, sometimes that hug turns into a "Thirteen" hug. So they're all getting closer and closer to the surface and I know now when I see the smile that lights up a room, that's from Eleven, but it's on Ron's face at times; so it's kind of neat. There's a way to go, but we're in it together. I'm a little bit afraid of how the little ones are going to react when I go to have my surgery, but I'll do some preparation work on that. One other neat thing is that now that we're living with my mother, the kids don't mind, coming out and giving me a hug when we're in the kitchen, and my mom is in the kitchen, or if the three of us happen to be in the living room at the same time. And, in fact, the little one, Seven, who likes to blow bubbles will walk by my mother and say, "Hello ma'am!" He's very polite and she talks back to him like he's a little seven-year-old and she just keeps saying to me, "Barbara, I can't believe it! The way he walks is different; the way he holds himself; the way he talks." So all of these little ones, from age seven all the way through age fourteen, plus Shadow are all very, very different. I haven't seen Fourteen in a while; I don't know what's going on with him. And I haven't seen Ten in a while: he's the one who had the car battery blow up in his face. Seven comes out to say hello fairly often and sometimes when Ron is tired and gives me a hug, Thirteen sneaks out and hugs me and Twelve nuzzles his head against my neck at the same time. Sometimes Eleven, Twelve and Thirteen all kind of combine together and now I'm hoping that Shadow will start to combine with them and feel more comfortable. So that's all I'll say right now about this, but I'll add a little bit more later.

Barbara explains the details of her back surgery, and that she has an appointment next Tuesday to determine when the surgery will take place. She explains the complexity of the surgery and it is clear that the word major should be with a capital

M regarding this complex procedure. She has an outstanding neurosurgeon to do the job. She explains also that it's quite an adjustment being out of work, but that she has to get used to it since she will not be able to function on a job for nearly a year.

Today's session with Ron proves monumental. Shadow comes out in my office and he is a whole different person than any of the other little Ronnies. His body is full of twitches and he talks in a soft muddled way with Barbara sitting next to him. His speech is so soft that I cannot distinguish what he is saying because of the softness and Barbara interprets or repeats what Ron is saying so that I will get the message. Shadow makes it clear that he is the depository for all of the feelings of all of Ron's little splinters. This is a key psychological factor and it shows that there is an integration process taking place. It is quite remarkable to see Shadow, and to see the different way he has of speaking from all of the other Ronnies and it is contributing to our therapeutic success that he is able to reveal Shadow. Shadow explains today that there are a lot of other things that happened to all the little kids, and he is nervous about everything coming out. He wonders why it is necessary to face the feelings and incidents that are completely repressed, but his actually coming out during a therapy session is testimony to the fact that he wants to get at all the old feelings.

After several months of therapy I feel privileged to witness the emergence of Shadow and to begin to understand this whole process. We are on the verge of still more success, and this is a very exciting situation. I ask Barbara if she will talk a little about what has been happening recently with Ron, Shadow and the other little Ronnies and she agrees:

Sure, I can talk about what happened yesterday. It was interesting that Ron started thinking back to what he and Dave had talked about in a previous session with Mr. Morgan's field having one special green grassy area (a childhood memory). We were all thinking that this had something to do with tombstones, but we were thinking about it from the wrong angle. Ron got very quiet, put his head back, relaxed, and tried to think about stuff. He got extremely quiet. I was sitting next to him and started to see his hand twitch a little bit and his shoulder twitch, so I put my hand on his hand and I said to Dave, "I think that Shadow is trying to come out." I just squeezed Ron's hand a little bit and he squeezed back and then I said very softly to him, "Shadow, it's OK. You can come out now if you want to talk to Mr. Johnson. You're very safe in here." Ron did a lot of twitching of his arms and shoulders and his head a little bit and I asked him, "Sweetheart, would you feel better if I put my arm around your shoulder, like we do at home?" And he sort of nodded and very quietly said, "Well, maybe. Maybe that would be good." So I moved over closer on Dave's loveseat, and put my arm around Ron's shoulder. He relaxed a little bit and then was just very, very quiet. So I said, "Honey, we're here with Mr. Johnson, do you want to say hello?" and a very soft voice said, "Hello." I then asked him, "Do you have anything that you want to talk about?" and he was very quiet for a while and Dave wanted to know how I could tell that Shadow was the one that had come out; Shadow had never come out when anybody else was nearby. I told him that I could tell by the way Ron/Shadow held himself and by the twitching that came beforehand. I can also tell from his voice, the way that he speaks and especially from his posture. He either curls his fingers around mine or makes the "I love you" sign-language symbol and presses it against my heart.

Dave said hello to Shadow and reassured him that he was in a safe place and that no one here was going to harm him. I repeated to Shadow that it was OK to talk to Mr. Johnson, that he was a very nice and kind man who was helping Uncle Ron, all the other little Ronnies, and me. Ron/Shadow snuggled a bit closer to me and very quietly started talking, mostly only loud enough so that I could hear him, so what I started to do was to repeat what he would say in a way that would make him feel like I was trying to make sure that I understood him, so that Dave could hear him because Shadow spoke so very quietly. At first Shadow said, "Other bad things with other kids" and I immediately thought, oh my God; his dad had something to do with sexual abuse to other children, until he spoke a bit further and said "Other kids have things happen and I have feelings." And I realized that when he was talking about the other kids, he was talking about all the other little Ronnies, the other "splinters."

A few minutes before Shadow came out, Dave and I had just learned that when Ron and his dad were driving along in their car one night, and Ron's dad was drunk, they went off the road, and of course his dad blamed Ron, and said "It's your fault that we went off the road." So after his dad got the car back on the road, he drove off and made Ron walk home in the pitch dark. It took him three hours to get there. Thinking along those lines, what Shadow referred to as "other bad things with other kids" were those types of things that happened to the other kids, things like being left alone in the dark along the side of a deserted road, or being chased through the woods at night. The other kids had things like that happen, and other things that I'm sure we'll learn about. A really interesting aspect was that he kept saying, "Other kids like Mr. Johnson." and "Why does Uncle Ron have to know about these? Better not to know than make Uncle Ron sad." And we said, "It's OK. Eventually when you feel you're ready, anything that you need to talk about, or that the others need to talk about, can come out, but you'll know when and you'll know how fast. Because if Uncle Ron doesn't know, then there'll always be a blank, and we want him to know everything. We want him to know the good things and the bad things." Shadow was quiet for a while and then he said "Yeah, other things happen. I hold feelings." He began to talk again about Mr. Morgan's field across the way and said that Mr. Morgan didn't like the kids to be around his pasture and scaring the cows, but it was a convenient way to get home from wherever they happened to be playing, or coming home from school. Little Shadow said that one time he could remember cutting across Mr. Morgan's pasture and Mr. Morgan catching him. He tried to get away and Mr. Morgan said, "No, wait, I want to talk to you; you stay right there!" and Mr. Morgan shut off the tractor and came over. He said, "You see that green area over there? Well, you know there are new rules now; the government won't let you have a family cemetery, but all of us in the family want to be buried on our own land. So that's why that whole area is nice and pretty and green and grassy, but I think I need to have somebody to help me take care of it. I'm going to go and get some headstones made and placed there so that it'll look like it's already a family cemetery. But you know, I need to have to have somebody help me take care of it and if you would like to help me do that, if you'd like to take care of it, you could use my tools; you could use my mower; you could use whatever of my equipment you needed to, and that would be something that you could do to get away from the house." Ron said, "Yeah, I'd like to do that." And he did. And then Mr. Morgan also said to him, "You know, I notice you spend a lot of time in the woods, and I have the feeling that you've maybe been sleeping in the woods at night." This was very hard for little Ron to admit to, and then Mr. Morgan said, "You know, if you ever need a bed, you can come and stay with Mrs. Morgan and me; we have an extra bed, and you can sleep at our house any time that you want to." Dave and I asked Shadow what he thought about that and he said that that was kind of nice and that Mr. Morgan was really nice. I don't think that Ron took him up on that offer of a warm bed as opposed to sleeping in his shelter in the woods; perhaps we'll find out whether he did or not. But, it was interesting to note that obviously even though Mr. Morgan's field and pasture and house were easily about the same distance as between Dave's office and the center of Bristol away, maybe a good mile away from Ron's house, Mr. Morgan obviously knew that something not so good was going on at Ron's house and he knew enough to ask and try and help him. So now we have the feeling that other people in town had to know that things were going on at Ron's house and perhaps we'll find out more about that when more of Ron's memories return.

Today's session with Ron proves to be a meaningful one. It takes him quite a while to relax and dissociate. His wife, Barbara, has to sit right next to him, prompting him quietly, and she has to have his left arm around him while he nestles into her upper body, head almost meeting head, or better yet, his head in between her shoulder and her head. Shadow puts his hand in Barbara's hand in the way that only Shadow can, fingers curled into fingers curled. One can tell that the dissociative behavior is in existence when Ron starts with his body and arm twitches, and at that point you know that Shadow is coming forward.

At this point in time, Ron is walking along a trail in the woods. I think that this might be close to either Little Frog Mountain or Big Frog Mountain, but I am not sure. The area is what's known as the Ocoee area. This is a Cherokee name for the mountainous area. Part of this land is the Cherokee National Forest and this forest separates the upper and lower parts of Fargo county in Georgia. The Cherokee reservation is in North Carolina. At some point in history, many, many years ago, one half of the remaining Cherokee nation lived on this reservation and the other half was sent to the reservation in Oklahoma. The path they walked to get there is known as the "Trail of Tears."

At this point, Ron sees himself sitting on a big rock. He has his backpack on and he is completely distraught and wanting to die. Ron has never been able to follow through with killing himself, but that does not stop him from wanting to die. We don't get very far, other than to capture Ron's mood of desperation. Soon Ron snaps out of his dissociation and it is quite obvious when this happens. It would be obvious to almost anybody because he physically flinches and jerks awake. One significant point does come out and that is that all the bad feelings that Ron has are discarded into Shadow, the holder of all Ron's feelings. When Ron regains consciousness, I explain to him that it is my feeling that when a person comes to terms with the fact that he or she wants to die, at that moment, he or she begins to die, in terms of feelings, that is. At this particular point, the individual perfects the art of emotional novocain, and gradually shuts off his feelings. Unfortunately, when one does this to him or herself, the mechanism shuts off ALL feelings and not only can the individual no longer feel angry and severely depressed, he or she just exists the same way as an automobile exists when put in neutral; the high and low gears do not work any longer. This is a particular kind of depression where one is not suicidal, and one cannot feel or enjoy the beat in a favorite musical tune, and one does not notice

90

sunset or sunrise. One does not notice the leaves changing colors during fall. One does not look at the first fall of snow of the winter and say, "Wow, this is beautiful!." In the case of the Dissociative Disorder, the bad feelings are compartmentalized into an identity. In this case, the feelings follow a trail of all the little Ronnies that lead to the main source of novocain that is Shadow. I explain again to Ron that, at this time of consciousness, that it is very healthy that his dissociative behavior is not leaving him driving in some part of the state and waking up not knowing who he is, or where he is, or how to get back home. As stated earlier sometimes this does occur with a Dissociative Disorder.

I explain to Ron that the integration process is taking place and that the little Ronnies are gradually disappearing. Today is only the second time in Ron's therapy that he permits me to witness the emergence of Shadow. I explain to Ron that he no longer needs to repress his feelings. He is in therapy, and I see him at least twice a week and he knows that if he needs to be seen five times a week, I will gladly permit that to occur. Once again I am encouraging Ron during consciousness to accept the fact that he can deal with his feelings as one whole person; that he does not need to dissociate, whether outside the office or in the office, but if he still needs to dissociate during therapy sessions, that is fine. However, we are working on dealing with reality, and I explain to Ron that he can learn to deal with these feelings within therapy, as a full-fledged and one hundred percent adult Ron. This is gradually taking place and we will see how fast we can move ahead without rushing things.

* * *

Chapter 15

Barbara's session today is an agonizing one. She has been planning on having

major back surgery and she is having difficulty also getting appointments specifically

for something called a discography, where the disc areas are injected with a special

dye for diagnostic reasons. She is willing to go all over the state to get the

necessary appointments, and the doctor doing the discography has offices in

Boston, New Haven and Bridgeport. She has scheduled an appointment all the way

down in Bridgeport, over an hour away. She doesn't care where she has to go, she

just wants to get the situation over with. She has been told that it could be

"relatively" minor surgery, like a Laminectomy, or it could also be major surgery

involving multi-level lumbar fusion. There certainly is an element of risk connected

with the major surgery. Barbara has an anxiety condition and because the degree of

anticipatory anxiety is very severe with anyone awaiting back surgery, her condition

has caused us to increase her medication as she waits for the various diagnostic procedures and eventual surgery to take place. Of course, complicating this situation is that she is only a couple of months out of her job after being terminated.

At the beginning of today's session Ron's wife Barbara explains the integration process that is taking place whereby all of Ron's personalities are merging gradually together to become one:

> *In the beginning there were Ronnies 7 through 13, and they were all distinct little individuals, but over the last several months, Twelve, who is always cold, has teamed up with Thirteen, who is always scared. When Twelve gives me a hug, he sort of nuzzles my neck and when Thirteen gives me a hug, it's a bear hug. Most of the time now I get the bear hug together with the nuzzle and they both seem to be coming out at the same time, but now Ron actually hugs me the same way without realizing it. Eleven was the one who would keep everything in order. He's started helping Twelve and Thirteen to not be sad and scared so much, so now sometimes all three of them seem to be there at the same time. Now Ron is smiling the smile that lights up a room like Eleven does. Thinking about Seven and Eight, Seven is the last one that remembers anything that was fun with his daddy, and Eight's memories emerge at the start of things going terribly wrong; but now it seems like Seven and Eight are starting to come together. They both have little giggles and little smiles and sometimes I can't tell which one is which until we talk a bit. All of them seem to be coming closer and closer to the surface. Shadow, who just appeared a couple of months ago, now will come out a little bit and he is starting to understand that this is actually 2003. The big breakthrough was our wedding anniversary. All of the little ones wrote things in a card and Shadow actually came out by himself and wrote "THANK YOU," and signed it with an "S."*

> *When we were in session the other day with Dave, Ron was remembering when he was a child finding a little baby bird on our sidewalk; he thought that the baby bird might be dead, but when he knelt down to check it, the little bird opened up its mouth. Ron's been dreaming about this little bird and had it on his mind, and the little Ronnies, Seven and Eight, were very worried about the bird. In one of his recent sessions, Ron started talking about this and realized that he really sees himself as the baby bird. This in itself is important because now he's able to deal with his feelings better, but what's even more important is that while he was speaking I could tell*

by his twitches and his mannerisms that he was anywhere from Eight to Thirteen; but he remembered the conversation! He felt like he was sitting back watching himself as one of the kids, as if watching a video of the whole thing. This was the one of the few times that he dissociated in session, brought out something, actually heard it as it was going on, and remembered it afterwards because he knew that he actually said it. So this is really neat! They're all closer and closer now to the surface. Eleven, Twelve, and Thirteen know almost everything that Ron does, so it's really great to see. The mannerisms that Ron has now are closer and closer to his little splinters. Most of what he recalled this time when he spoke – it was him talking as himself, and he was pretty much himself all the way through. I could tell by his twitches that the "little ones" were there, especially right near the end I know one of the little ones came out, but yet Ron knew everything. He was able to go back without becoming the little one and actually acting it out.

*   *   *

Chapter 16

Barbara reports to the group that she has to have major back surgery and may be out of work for a year. Barbara and Ron have been through such horrendous difficulties in the past year, that one cannot blame her for being depressed. She deals with Ron's Dissociative Identity Disorder and now he is dealing with his problem of vertigo, in which he is going to require physical therapy to desensitize him against the symptoms. The two of them keep rolling with the punches, and Barbara reports to the group how the integration process is taking place with Ron and all of his different little Ronnies gradually merging into one. She and Ron both see this happening and are thrilled by it. Ron's concern at this point is with his vertigo. He is missing days at work and his boss is not feeling too happy about it, so we have to see how the physical therapy assists him.

Barbara explains where she and Ron stand with the process of moving back into Barbara's mom's home. They cannot afford to keep their apartment while Barbara is out of work and because she may be out of work for more than a year due to her upcoming back surgery, they need to do something to cut expenses. The situation is going to be a tricky one. In the past, Barbara's mother would get teed off about something in the refrigerator missing that she had bought for herself. Barbara and Ron are going to have a little private area in the basement of the home with a TV set so that there is some separation between the two of them and her mom. I suggest to Barbara that they get a refrigerator downstairs so there would be no issue of who's food is whose. In addition, Barbara's mom is becoming increasingly disabled with her bad back and troubled legs. I think that there is going to be an interesting set of dynamics that will take place between mother, daughter and son-in-law. At times things can get tense and nasty with her mom. Now that Barbara's mom has been into my office for a session with me, just to talk about and understand Ron's illness a little bit better, the ice has been broken and it will be easier to get Ron, Barbara, Barbara's mom, and myself together for family sessions, if we need them. That certainly will be a plus.

* * *

Chapter 17

I will see Ron tonight in session; I am staying an additional forty-five minutes past
my usual end of the day to see him because he has been working fifty or sixty hours
a week at the bowling alley because of another key employee's illness. Apparently
Ron's vertigo is clearing up bit by bit. I have not heard any complaints about it from
him or Barbara, so whatever vestibular therapy is like, it appears to be making a
dent in the problem. Barbara continues to build rapport with her mother as they plan
to move into her home since they will not be able to afford their apartment.

In Ron's session today, he goes back to a piece of property way to the rear of his
home, following a creek that he does not know the name of, and he enters what he
calls the Morgan property, just on the edge of the Hilliard property. At this point,
what he sees in his mind, not in reality, is a black curtain that he should not or
cannot go beyond. My interpretation of the black curtain is that he is being kept from

taking a look at certain feelings that will erupt should he enter the Hilliard property. In my mind and verbally to Ron, I ask him, "Are you afraid of finding another body or something like that?" He says that he doesn't know, but he doesn't think so. After further relaxation time, Ron is able to break down the black curtain and in the stream he sees a dead dog. The dog had been shot. He recognizes the dog as Ben, one of his favorite dogs; his family kept several of them. He, I believe, picks up the dog and puts it into something whereby he can carry it home, but he is upset by the fact that he had talked to his father about Ben being missing and his father didn't have anything to say about it. Apparently there also had been a couple of other dogs missing from the property, namely two of the collies.

Ron gets into a confrontation with his father over the dead dog. At this time, Ron is about fourteen years old and at this age he, more often than not, stands up to his father and faces him and confronts him with situations that he is not happy with. Ron is not a little tyke anymore. Ron's dad tells him that he owes him an explanation for nothing. Ron is extremely upset, but cannot get anything out of his father. One of the things that disturbs Ron the most, in this confrontation and in others lately, is that his mother is there saying, "Ron, don't talk back to your father." There are several reasons for the black curtain, not merely the killing of Ben. I think the main issue is that Ron's mother is continuously taking part in not considering Ron's feelings and abandoning him as a nurturing mother. Sitting in the chair in this therapist's office, it is clear to me that at this time, as a fourteen year old boy, Ron's feelings of hatred and guilt are peaking towards his father as well as towards his mother. Ron has more respect for the directness of his father's approach than he does for the devious, manipulative quality of his mother's abandonment of him. Once again, Mom has faltered on her promise to get away from Dad. It is now clear to Ron, at age fourteen, that she has no intention of doing so. The black curtain is simply a manifestation of a territory which Ron does not want to explore, namely the realization that he does not have a place of importance in his mother's heart and that is a devastating thought.

Conclusion

It is now February 2008, and the complexities of Ron's multi-personalities are diminishing by leaps and bounds. Therapy four or five times per week two years ago has resulted in the integration process taking place. Ron is very much one whole person. It has been several months since we have seen one of "the kids" completely take over Ron's existence. However, when he is under extreme stress, he will regress when he is alone with Barbara and do a little "switching" into a "kid" identity. This lasts for only a few minutes and is not at all disruptive to his functioning.

Therapy continues with Ron on a less frequent basis. It is very healthy that Ron's employment keeps him so busy. When we started therapy five years ago, he was completely dominated and controlled by one or another of his "splinters" and far from able to work. Our sessions at this point are in "the here and now" and it is not required by his illness to dissociate in order to get at feelings. The integration of all the personalities into one means that all unconscious material is now conscious, and therefore more easily controlled and channeled.

I have asked Ron to put into writing what his life is like today and how he is dealing with his Dissociative Identity Disorder. What follows are his own words.

When Mr. Johnson first broached the idea of a book including my struggle with Dissociative Identity Disorder, I was hit with both excitement and trepidation. I wasn't at all sure if I could handle seeing all I have lived through in print, and I was worried about my remaining family members' reaction to the real story of my life described in these new memories.

Then I realized that this is an opportunity to help validate not only my experience but also other peoples' experiences with this disorder. There is a stigma of skepticism and outright dismissal around this disorder that has to be lifted. Until this happens, there are other people in the world who will not receive the treatment they need and the respect they deserve by dealing with DID on a daily basis for most of their lives.

The bottom line is this: Dissociative Identity Disorder (a.k.a. Multiple Personality Disorder) is real. It does exist. I know – I spend every day with it. It takes every ounce of my emotional energy to get up every morning, go to work and come home to face life's struggles which, while routine for most people, often leave me exhausted and dreading getting up the next morning to do it all over again.

A therapist I met early in my journey, and for whom I have a great deal of respect, once told me that "DIDers," as she termed us, are the true survivors of the mental health world. As young children, we are not experienced enough to understand what is happening to us and so we "store away" the bad things heaped on us and lock those memories away so that we don't have to suffer with them.

This is a great mechanism for a child, helping him cope with unimaginable abuse in a way that keeps his mind intact, but compartmentalized. However, those experiences can't stay locked up forever, and when the trigger that finally releases them comes along, suddenly the world is turned inside out. What should be 20- or 30-year-old memories are to us things that were done to us yesterday. When a therapist or lay person says "Those things happened long ago. Drop them and move on," they are exposing themselves as not really understanding the ordeal we face.

I have been very fortunate. I have learned coping skills that help me function in the real world as a productive member of society. I have a fulltime job that requires skilled hands and concentration in a sometimes hazardous environment. I have a loving wife who has given me more support than I thought possible when I first became afflicted. Fortune has given me a therapist whose kind and gentle brand of therapy has helped me become whole again.

But don't be misled. I struggle with this disorder every single minute of every single day. There isn't a cure for DID, just as with most emotional disorders. I still dissociate on occasion, but have trained myself to do so only in safe places and at appropriate times, at home or in Mr. Johnson's office. Every day I have to be on my guard to not allow a random incident or a stressful environment to catch me off guard.

And yet, and this may sound odd, I'm thankful for having set out on this path. Memories are important, good and bad. They make us who we are, and if forced to choose, I wouldn't throw the bad ones away.

One thing that still happens to me, and I hope always will, is that I am discovering new wonders in the world. I get excited to see a bird's nest with eggs in it and realizing that new life is coming soon. I see the trees and marvel at how many shades of green there are. Simply flying a kite can make me happy and giddy as a schoolboy. I appreciate all of life's little miracles, miracles that I couldn't see before my "splinters" came calling. Emotions that had died an early death have been resurrected.

The horrendous things I had to remember have actually let me learn there are wonders to be seen in the little things. This is the gift my "kids" have given me, and I thank them every day for that gift.

I want to thank my wife of 28 years, Mr. Johnson, and my fellow patients for all the help they have given me. I would not have succeeded as much as I have without them. They are the ones that have made it possible for me to live in the real world and the here and now. It scares me to think where I could have landed when my life took this turn – "But for the Grace of God..."

It should be mentioned that Ron and I cooperated in discussions with the sheriff who covers the county where Ron lived during his traumatic years. The effort was to substantiate Ron's memories with "hard evidence," such as bodily remains or missing person reports. We came up batting zero. Record keeping decades ago was not thorough in "Hick Town." The shack that Ron grew up in didn't even have a street address, and new housing developments and miles of bramble bushes made searching for bodies impossible. We even secured aerial photographs of the area, but they didn't help at all. Several decades of Ron's life had passed, but not the scars, which are still present.

15595839R00059

Made in the USA
Lexington, KY
05 June 2012